Also by Mark Myers

A Smarter Way to Learn Python

Mark Myers

Learn it faster.
Remember it longer.

If you embrace this method of learning, you'll get the hang of Python in less time than you might expect. And the knowledge will stick.

You'll catch onto concepts quickly.

You'll be less bored, and might even be excited. You'll certainly be motivated.

You'll feel confident instead of frustrated.

You'll remember the lessons long after you close the book.

Is all this too much for a book to promise? Yes, it is. Yet I can make these promises and keep them, because this isn't just a book. It's a book plus almost a thousand interactive online exercises.

You're going to learn by doing. You'll read a chapter, then practice with the exercises. That way, the knowledge gets embedded in your memory so you don't forget it. Instant feedback corrects your mistakes like a one-on-one teacher.

I've done my best to write each chapter so it's easy for anyone to understand, but it's the exercises that are going to turn you into a real Python coder.

Cognitive research shows that reading alone doesn't buy you much long-term retention. Even if you read a book a second or even a third time, things won't improve much, according to research.

And forget highlighting or underlining. Marking up a book gives us the illusion that we're engaging with the material, but studies show that it's an exercise in self-deception. It doesn't matter how much yellow you paint on the pages, or how many times you review the highlighted material. By the time you get to Chapter 50, you'll have forgotten most of what you highlighted in Chapter 1.

This all changes if you read less and do more—if you read a short passage and then immediately put it into practice. Washington University researchers say that being asked to retrieve information increases long-term retention by four hundred percent. That may seem implausible, but by the time you finish this book, I think you'll believe it.

Practice also makes learning more interesting.

Trying to absorb long passages of technical material puts you to sleep and kills your motivation. Ten minutes of reading followed by fifteen minutes of challenging practice keeps you awake and spurs you on.

And it keeps you honest.

If you *only* read, it's easy to kid yourself that you're learning more than you are. But when you're challenged to produce the goods, there's a moment of truth. You *know* that you know—or that you don't. When you find out that you're a little shaky on this point or that, you can review the material, then re-do the exercise. That's all it takes to master this book from beginning to end—and to build a solid foundation of Python knowledge.

I've talked with many readers who say they thought they had a problem understanding technical concepts. But what looked like a comprehension problem was really a retention problem. If you get to Chapter 50 and everything you studied in Chapter 1 has faded from memory, how can you understand Chapter 50, which depends on your knowing Chapter 1 cold? The read-then-practice approach embeds the concepts of each chapter in your long-term memory, so you're prepared to tackle material in later chapters that builds on top of those concepts. When you're able to remember what you read, you'll find that you learn Python quite readily.

I hope you enjoy this learning approach. And I hope you build on it to become a terrific coder.

How to use this book

This isn't a book quite like any you've ever owned before, so a brief user manual might be helpful.

- **Study, practice, then rest.** If you're intent on mastering the fundamentals of Python, as opposed to just getting a feel for the language, work with this book and the online exercises in a 15-to-25-minute session, then take a break. Study a chapter for 5 to 10 minutes. Immediately go to the online link given at the end of each chapter and code for 10 to 15 minutes, practicing the lesson until you've coded everything correctly. Then take a walk.

- **Do the coding exercises on a physical keyboard.** A mobile device can be ideal for reading, but it's no way to code. Very, very few Web developers would attempt to do their work on a phone. The same thing goes for learning to code. Theoretically, most of the interactive exercises could be done on a mobile device. But the idea seems so perverse that I've disabled online practice on tablets, readers, and phones.

- **If you have an authority problem, try to get over it.** When you start doing the exercises, you'll find that I can be a pain about insisting that you get every little detail right. For example, if you omit spaces where spaces belong, the program monitoring your work will tell you the code isn't correct, even though it might still run perfectly. Do I insist on having everything just so because I'm a control freak? No, it's because I have to place a limit on harmless maverick behavior in order to automate the exercises. If I were to grant you as much freedom as you might like, creating the algorithms that check your work would be, for me, a project of frightening proportions. Besides, learning to write code with fastidious precision helps you learn to pay close attention to details, a fundamental requirement for coding in any language.

- **Subscribe, temporarily, to my formatting biases.**
  Current code formatting is like seventeenth-century spelling.
  Everyone does it his own way. There are no universally
  accepted standards. But the algorithms that check your work
  when you do the interactive exercises need standards. They
  can't grant you the latitude that a human teacher could,
  because, let's face it, algorithms aren't that bright. So I've
  had to settle on certain conventions. All of the conventions
  I teach are embraced by a large segment of the coding
  community, so you'll be in good company. But that doesn't
  mean you'll be married to my formatting biases forever.
  When you start coding projects, you'll soon develop your
  own opinions or join an organization that has a stylebook.
  Until then, I'll ask you to make your code look like my code.

The language you're learning here

Python is a popular, 30-year-old general purpose programming language created by Guido van Rossum. Compared with some other languages, it's reasonably easy to learn, and it's relatively easy to read. Python is often used to teach beginners the fundamentals of programming.

1
print

In Python, the command **print** tells the program to display words or numbers on the screen. Here's a line of code that tells Python to display the words "Hello, World!"

```
print("Hello, World!")
```

print is a *keyword*—that is, a word that has special meaning for Python. It means, "Display what's inside the parentheses." Note that **print** isn't capitalized. If you capitalize it, the program won't run.

The parentheses are a special requirement of Python, one that you'll soon get used to. You'll be typing parentheses over and over again, in all kinds of Python statements.

In coding, the quoted text in the line above—"Hello, World!"—is called a *text string* or simply a *string*. The name makes sense: it's a string of characters.

When Python displays a string on the screen, the quotation marks don't display. They're only in your code to tell Python that it's dealing with a string.

Note that the opening parenthesis is jammed up against the keyword *print*, and the opening quotation mark is hugging the opening parenthesis. You *could* space it out, writing...

```
print ( "Hello, World!" )
```

But I want you to learn the style conventions of Python, so I'll ask you to omit spaces when it's the conventional thing to do.

Find the interactive coding exercises for this chapter at:
http://www.ASmarterWayToLearn.com/python/1.html

2
Variables for Strings

Please memorize the following facts.

- My name is Mark.

- My nationality is U.S.

Now that you've memorized my name and nationality, I won't have to repeat them again. If I say to you, "You probably know other people who have my name," you'll know I'm referring to "Mark."

If I ask you whether my nationality is the same as yours, I won't have to ask, "Is your nationality the same as U.S.?" I'll ask, "Is your nationality the same as my nationality?" You'll remember that when I say "my nationality," I'm referring to "U.S.", and you'll compare your nationality with "U.S.", even though I haven't said "U.S." explicitly.

In these examples, the terms **my name** and **my nationality** work the same way Python *variables* do. **my name** refers to a particular value, "Mark." In the same way, a variable refers to a particular value. You could say that **my name** is a variable that refers to the string "Mark."

A variable is created this way:

```
name = "Mark"
```

Now the variable **name** refers to the text string "Mark".

Note that it was my choice to call it **name**. I could have called it **my_name**, **xyz**, **lol**, or something else. It's up to me how to name my variables, within limits. More on those limits later.

With the string "Mark" assigned to the variable **name**, my Python code doesn't have to specify "Mark" again. Whenever Python encounters **name**, Python knows that it's a variable that refers to "Mark".

For example, if you write...

```
name = "Mark"
print(name)
```

...Python displays...

Mark

The value that a variable refers to can change.

Let's go back to the original examples, the facts I asked you to memorize. These facts can change, and if they do, the terms **my name** and **my nationality** will refer to new values.

I could go to court and change my name to Ace. Then my name is no longer Mark. If I want you to address me correctly, I'll have to tell you that my name is now Ace. After I tell you that, you'll know that my name doesn't refer to the value it used to refer to (Mark), but refers to a new value (Ace).

If I acquire U.K. citizenship, my nationality is no longer U.S. It's U.K. If I want you to know my nationality, I'll have to tell you that it is now U.K. After I tell you that, you'll know that my nationality doesn't refer to the original value, "U.S.", but now refers to a new value, U.K.

Python variables can also change.

If I code...

```
name = "Mark"
```

...**name** refers to "Mark". Then I come along later and code the line...

```
name = "Ace"
```

Before I coded the new line, if I asked Python to print **name**, it displayed...

Mark

But that was then.

Now if, having written...

```
name = "Ace"
```

...if I write...

```
print(name)
```

...Python displays...

Ace

A variable can have any number of values, but only one at a time.
Python variable names have no inherent meaning to Python.

In English, words have meaning. You can't use just any word to communicate. I can say, "My name is Mark," but, if I want to be understood, I can't say, "My floogle is Mark." That's nonsense.

But with variables, Python is blind to semantics. You can use just any word (as long as it doesn't break the rules of variable-naming, which I'll cover later). From Python's point of view...

```python
floogle = "Mark"
```

...is just as good as...

```python
name = "Mark"
```

If you write...

```python
floogle = "Mark"
```

...then write…

```python
print(floogle)
```

…Python displays...

Mark

Within limits, you can name variables anything you want, and Python won't care.

```python
lesson_author = "Mark"
guy_who_keeps_saying_his_own_name = "Mark"
x = "Mark"
```

Python's blindness to meaning notwithstanding, when it comes to variable names, you'll want to give your variables meaningful names, because it'll help you and other coders understand your code.

Again, the syntactic difference between variables and text strings is that variables are never enclosed in quotes, and text strings are always enclosed in quotes.

It's always...

```
last_name = "Smith"
city_of_origin = "New Orleans"
aussie_greeting = "g'Day"
```

If it's an alphabet letter or word, and it isn't enclosed in quotes, and it isn't a keyword that has special meaning for Python, like **print**, it's a variable.

If it's some characters enclosed in quotes, it's a text string.

If you haven't noticed, let me point out the spaces between the variable and the equal sign, and between the equal sign and the value.

```
nickname = "Bub"
```

These spaces are a style choice rather than a legal requirement. But I'll ask you to include them in your code throughout the practice exercises.

In the last chapter you learned to write...

```
print("Hello, World!")
```

When the code executes, Python displays **Hello World!** on the screen.

But what if you wrote these two statements instead (the line numbers are added automatically by the editing program; they're not part of the code):

```
1 thanx = "Thanks for your input!"
2 print(thanx)
```

Instead of placing a text string inside the parentheses of the **print** statement, the code above first assigns the text string to a variable, **thanx**. Then it places the variable, not the string, inside the parentheses. Because Python always substitutes the value for the variable, Python displays—not the variable name **thanx**—but the text to which it refers, "Thanks for your input!" **Thanks for your input!** displays.

In the example above, notice that each statement is on a separate line.

I mentioned that you have to follow certain rules for naming variables. One that I've already covered: You can never enclose a variable name in quotation marks.

Here's a second rule: Variable names can't have spaces in them. **country of origin** is not a legal variable name.

It has to be…

countryoforigin

…or, better for readability…

country_of_origin

I'll cover a few more rules for naming variables shortly.

Find the interactive coding exercises for this chapter at http://www.ASmarterWayToLearn.com/python/2.html

3
Variables for Numbers

A string isn't the only thing you can assign to a variable. You can also assign a number.

```
weight = 150
```

Having coded the statement above, whenever you write **weight** in your code, Python knows you mean 150. You can use this variable in math calculations.

If you ask Python to add 25 to **weight**...

```
weight + 25
```

...Python, remembering that **weight** refers to 150, will come up with the sum 175.

Unlike a string, a number is not enclosed in quotes. That's how Python knows it's a number that it can do math on and not a text string, like a ZIP code, that it handles as text.

But then, since it's not enclosed in quotes, how does Python know it's not a variable? Well, because a number can't be used as a variable name. If it's a number, Python rejects it as a variable. So it must be a number.

If you enclose a number in quotation marks, it's a string. Python can't do addition on it. It can do addition only on numbers not enclosed in quotes.

Now look at this code.

```
1  original_num = 23
2  new_num = original_num + 7
```

In the second statement in the code above, Python substitutes the number 23 when it encounters the variable **original_num**. It adds 7 to 23. And it assigns the result, 30, to the variable **new_num**.

Python can also do a calculation made up of nothing but variables. For example...

```
1   original_num = 23
2   num_to_be_added = 7
3   new_num = original_num + num_to_be_added
```

The variable **new_num** now has a value of 30.
A variable can be used in calculating its own new value.

```
1 original_num = 90
2 original_num = original_num + 10
```

The variable **original_num** now has a value of 100.
If you enclose a number in quotation marks and add 7...

```
1   original_num = "23"
2   new_num = original_num + 7
```

...it won't work, because Python can't sum a string and a number..

Note that a variable name can be the name of a number variable or a string variable. From Python's point of view, there's nothing in a name that denotes one kind of variable or another. In fact, a variable can start out as one type of variable, then become another type of variable.

You could write..

```
your_age = "21"
```

...and the variable **your_age** refers to a string. You can't do math on it.

But then if you write...

```
your_age = 21
```

..the variable **your_age** no longer refers to a string. It refers to a number. You can do math on it.

I've told you that a variable name can't be a number. But you can *include* numbers in a variable name — as long as you don't *begin* the name with a number. The statement...

```
1st_prime_number = 2
```

...is illegal, thanks to that initial **1** in the variable name.

But this variable name, where the **1** comes later in the name, is legal...

```
prime_number_that_comes1st = 2
```

In this chapter's examples, the numbers I assigned to variables were *integers* — whole numbers like 2, 47, 0, and -5. You can also assign *floats* to variables— numbers like 1.7, -.005, and 1.00009.

Find the interactive coding exercises for this chapter at http://www.ASmarterWayToLearn.com/python/3.html

4
Math expressions: Familiar operators

You've already used Python to make some simple calculations, like 2 + 2.

The programming term for a calculation is *math expression*. Familiar operators in math expressions are **+** (add), **-** (subtract), ***** (multiply), and **/** (divide).

As you've seen, instead of assigning a number to a variable...

```
popular_number = 4
```

...you can assign the result of a math expression to the variable...

```
popular_number = 2 + 2
```

Python makes the calculation 2 + 2 and assigns the result to the variable. In the statement above, **popular_number** is assigned the sum of 2 + 2—the number 4.

You can write:

```
print(2 + 2)
```

This displays **4** on the screen.

Here's a statement that subtracts 24 from 12, assigning the result, -12, to the variable.

```
loss = 12 - 24
```

This one assigns the product of 3 times 12—the result is 36—to the variable.

```
dozens = 3 * 12
```

This one assigns 12 divided by 4—the result is 3—to the variable.

```
popular_number = 12 / 4
```

In the next one, the float .075 is assigned to the variable **num**. Then the integer 200 is added to the variable, and the sum, 200.075, is assigned to a second variable, **total**. As usual, you can mix variables and numbers.

```
1 num = .075
2 total = num + 200
```

You can also do a calculation using an expression containing nothing but variables.

```
1 num = 10
2 another_num = 1.5
3 sum_of_numbers = num + another_num
```

In the statement above, the variable **sum_of_numbers** winds up with a value of 11.5.

Find the interactive coding exercises for this chapter at
http://www.ASmarterWayToLearn.com/python/4.html

5
Variable Names Legal and Illegal

You've already learned three rules about naming a variable:
1. You can't enclose it in quotation marks.
2. You can't have any spaces in it.
3. It can't be a number or begin with a number.

In addition, a variable can't be any of Python's *reserved* words, also known as keywords—the special words that act as programming instructions, like **print**.

Here's a list of them.

and	False	not
as	finally	or
assert	for	pass
break	from	print
class	global	raise
continue	if	return
def	import	True
del	in	try
elif	is	while
else	lambda	with
except	None	yield
	nonlocal	

You don't need to memorize the list. If you accidentally try to use one of the reserved words as a variable name, Python will refuse it and tell you that you've made a syntax error. However, it won't specify that it's a variable-naming error, so keep this list in mind.

Here are the rest of the rules for naming variables:

- A variable name can contain only lowercase letters, uppercase letters, numbers, and underscores.

- Though a variable name can't be any of Python's keywords, it can *contain* any of those keywords.

- Capital letters are fine, but be careful. Variable names are case-sensitive. A **rose** with a lowercase **r** is not a **Rose** with an uppercase **R**. If you assign the string "Floribundas" to the variable **rose**, and then ask Python for the value assigned to **Rose**, you'll come up empty.

- Python's governing body recommends breaking up multi-word variables with underscores. That's what I'll ask you to do with your own variable names. It'll make them more readable, and you'll be less likely to get variables mixed up.

Examples:

```
user_response
user_response_time
user_response_time_limit
```

Make your variable names descriptive so it's easier to figure out what your code means when you or someone else comes back to it three weeks or a year from now. Generally, **user_name** is better than **x**, and **fave_breed** is better than **fav_brd**, though the shorter names are perfectly legal. You should balance readability with conciseness, though. **best_supporting_actress_in_a_drama_or_comedy** is a model of clarity, but may be too much for most of us to type or read. You might want to shorten it.

Note: In this book and the exercises, I sometimes use variable names like **x**, **y**, and **z** to simplify teaching points.

Find the interactive coding exercises for this chapter at http://www.ASmarterWayToLearn.com/python/5.html

6
Math expressions: Unfamiliar operators

Now we come to a couple of operators that may be new to you.
Check this out:

```
whats_left_over = 10 % 3
```

`%` is the *modulo operator*. It divides one number by another number, but doesn't give you the result of the division. It gives you the remainder after the first number is divided by the second number. If you divide 10 by 3, the remainder is 1. So in the example above, **whats_left_over** has a value of 1.

If one number divides evenly into another, the modulo statement assigns 0 to the variable, since there is no remainder. In the following statement, 0 is assigned to the variable.

```
whats_left_over = 9 % 3
```

Here's a second operator.
Suppose you want to increase the value of a variable by 1. You could write…

```
age = age + 1
```

The statement increases the value of the variable **age** by 1. If the variable started off with a value of 54, for example, it now has a value of 55.

Here's a shorthand way of doing the same thing…

```
age += 1
```

Again, if the original value of **age** was 54, its new value is 55.
In the following code, age winds up with a value of 62.

```
age = 12
age += 50
```

You can use the same kind of shorthand for other operators, too. In the following code, **age** winds up with a value of 10.

```
1  age = 12
2  age -= 2
```

In the following code, **age** winds up with a value of 36.

```
1  age = 12
2  age *= 3
```

Don't forget that you can always use a variable instead of a number. In the following code, **age** winds up with a value of 15.

```
1  age = 12
2  amount_to_increment = 3
3  age += amount_to_increment
```

Find the interactive coding exercises for this chapter at http://www.ASmarterWayToLearn.com/python/6.html

7
Math expressions: Eliminating ambiguity

Complex arithmetic expressions can pose a problem, one that students face in high school algebra. Look at this example and tell me what the value of **total_cost** is.

```
total_cost = 1 + 3 * 4
```

The value of **total_cost** varies, depending on the order in which you do the arithmetic. If you begin by adding 1 + 3, then multiply the sum by 4, **total_cost** has a value of 16. But if you go the other way and start by multiplying 3 by 4, then add 1 to the product, you get 13.

In Python, as in algebra, the ambiguity is cleared up by precedence rules. As in algebra, the rule that applies here is that multiplication operations are completed before addition operations. So **total_cost** has the value of 13.

But you don't have to memorize Python's complex precedence rules. You can finesse the issue by using parentheses to eliminate ambiguity. Parentheses override all the other precedence rules. They force Python to complete operations enclosed by parentheses before completing any other operations.

When you use parentheses to make your intentions clear to Python, it also makes your code easier to grasp, both for other coders and for you when you're trying to understand your own code a year down the road. In this statement, the parentheses tell Python to first multiply 3 by 4, then add 1. The result: 13.

```
total_cost = 1 + (3 * 4)
```

If I move the parentheses, the arithmetic is done in a different order. In this next statement, the placement of the parentheses tells Python to first add 1 and 3, then multiply by 4. The result is 16.

```
total_cost = (1 + 3) * 4
```

Here's another example.

```
result_of_computation = (2 * 4) * 4 + 2
```

By placing the first multiplication operation inside parentheses, you've told Python to do that operation first. But then what? Is it…

- Multiply 2 by 4—that's 8—by 4—that's 32—then add 2 to it to get 34?

Or is it...

- Multiply 2 by 4—that's 8—by the sum of 4 and 2—that's 6—to get 48?

The solution is more parentheses.

If you want the second multiplication to be done before the 2 is added, write this...

```
result_of_computation = ((2 * 4) * 4) + 2
```

But if you want the product of 2 times 4 to be multiplied by the number you get when you total 4 and 2, write this...

```
result_of_computation = (2 * 4) * (4 + 2)
```

Find the interactive coding exercises for this chapter at http://www.ASmarterWayToLearn.com/python/7.html

8
Concatenating text strings

In Chapter 1 you learned to display a string on the screen, coding it this way.

```
print("Hello, World!")
```

In Chapter 2, you learned that you could use a variable to do the same thing .

```
1 greeting = "Hello, World!"
2 print(greeting)
```

But suppose you wanted to break the greeting into two parts, and assign each part to a separate variable, like this:

```
1 greeting = "Hello"
2 addressee = "World"
```

You tell Python to combine the two strings this way:

```
whole_greeting = greeting + addressee
```

It's called *concatenation*. All it takes is a plus sign.
Now, if you code…

```
print(whole_greeting)
```

…Python displays **HelloWorld**
That's not quite what we want, so let's add some more concatenation…

```
1 greeting = "Hello"
2 separators = ", "
3 addressee = "World"
4 punc = "!"
5 whole_greeting = greeting + separators + addressee + punc
6 print(whole_greeting)
```

Python displays **Hello, World!**

In the code above, I assigned the four parts of the whole greeting to four different variables. Then I concatenated them and assigned the combination to the variable **whole_greeting**.

Python is happy to concatenate strings as well as variables…

```
whole_greeting = "Hello, " + "World!"
```

…or a combination of variables and strings…

```
whole_greeting = "Hello" + separators + "World" + punc
```

You don't have to assign the result of a concatenation to a variable. This would work:

```
print("Hello, " + "World!")
```

So would this:

```
print(greeting + separators + addressee + punc)
```

…or this:

```
print("Hello" + separators + "World" + punc)
```

You can use the plus sign to sum numbers, and you can use it to concatenate strings. But you can't use the plus sign to combine strings and numbers. If you write this code, you get an error message:

```
print("The sum of 2 plus 2 is " + 4)
```

However, if you make that number a string, it'll work…

```
print("The sum of 2 plus 2 is " + "4")
```

Python displays **The sum of 2 plus 2 is 4**

Find the interactive coding exercises for this chapter at http://www.ASmarterWayToLearn.com/python/8.html

9
if statements

Suppose you want to know whether the string assigned to the variable **species** is "cat."

This is the code.

```
1 if species == "cat":
2    print("Yep, it's cat.")
```

If the string "cat" has been assigned to the variable **species**, Python displays the message **Yep, it's cat.** If the string "cat" hasn't been assigned to the variable **species**, nothing happens.

Let's break down the code.

It begins with the keyword **if**. Note that **if** is all lowercase. If you write **If** instead of **if**, it won't work. You'll get an error message.

Note that it's two equal signs, **==**, not one. One equal sign, **=**, can only be used to assign a value to a variable, as in...

```
species = "cat"
```

Whenever you're testing whether one thing is the same as another, the operator has to be **==**. Otherwise, you'll get an error message.

The first line ends with a colon.

```
1 if species == "cat":
```

If the test passes—if the string "cat" has been assigned to the variable **species**—you tell Python what to do. You put this on its own line, and you indent the line one tab:

```
1 if species == "cat":
2    print("Yep, it's cat.")
```

You can make any number of things happen when the answer to the **if** question is "yes." Each thing that happens gets its own line. And each line is indented.

```
1 if species == "cat":
2    status = "ok"
3    kingdom = "animal"
4    print("Yep, it's cat.")
```

There are other things you can test, including numbers. It works the same way…

```
1 if 2 + 2 == 4:
2    print("Everything makes sense.")
```

That test, of course, will always come out true, and the message will be displayed.

Here's another one, that might not always come out true.

```
1 if number_of_husbands == 1:
2    print("So far so good.")
```

In Python, indents aren't just for pretty formatting. They have meaning for Python. They aren't optional. In general, any lines of code that take their orders from a line that ends in a colon are indented. Example:

```
1 if number_of_husbands == 1:
2    print("So far so good.")
3    print("Congratulations.")
4    print("All done")
```

In the code above, lines 2 and 3 execute only if the **if** test in line 1 passes. Their execution is dependent on what happens in line 1, so they're indented. Line 4 executes no matter what. It runs independently of line 1, so it isn't indented.

What I'm saying here isn't strictly accurate. Later on you'll see some code that doesn't quite fit what I'm saying. But it's a handy way to think of indents in Python. As a rule of thumb: indent after a colon.

Find the interactive coding exercises for this chapter at:
http://www.ASmarterWayToLearn.com/python/9.html

10
Comparison operators

Let's talk a little more about **==**. It's a type of *comparison operator*, specifically it's the *equality operator*. As you learned in the last chapter, you use it to compare two things to see if they're equal.

You can use the equality operator to compare a variable with a string, a variable with a number, a variable with a math expression, or a variable with a variable. And you can use the equality operator to compare various combinations. All of the following are legal first lines in *if* statements:

```
if full_name == "Mark" + " " + "Myers":
if full_name == first_name + " " + "Myers":
if full_name == first_name + " " + last_name:
if total_cost == 81.50 + 135:
if total_cost == materials_cost + 135:
if total_cost == materials_cost + labor_cost:
if x + y == a - b:
```

When you're comparing strings, the equality operator is case-sensitive. "Rose" does not equal "rose."

Another comparison operator, **!=**, is the opposite of **==**. It means is *not* equal to.

```
1 if your_ticket_number != 487208:
2   print("Better luck next time.")
```

Like **==**, the not-equal operator can be used to compare numbers, strings, variables, math expressions, and combinations.

Like **==**, string comparisons using the not-equal operator are case-sensitive. It's true that "Rose" **!=** "rose".

Here are 4 more comparison operators, usually used to compare numbers.

> is greater than

< is less than

>= is greater than or equal to

<= is less than or equal to

In the examples below, all the conditions are true.

```
if 1 > 0:
if 0 < 1:
if 1 >= 0:
if 1 >= 1:
if 0 <= 1:
if 1 <= 1:
```

Find the interactive coding exercises for this chapter at
http://www.ASmarterWayToLearn.com/python/10.html

11
else and *elif* statements

The *if* statements you've coded so far have been all-or-nothing. If the condition tested true, something happened. If the condition tested false, nothing happened.

Often, you want something to happen either way. For example:

```
1 if species == "cat":
2   print("Yep, it's cat.")
3 if species != "cat":
4   print("Nope, not cat.")
```

In this example, we have two *if* statements, one testing for "cat," and another testing for not-"cat". So all cases are covered, with one message or another displaying, depending on what the value of the variable **species** is.

The code works, but it's more verbose than necessary, and a little nutty. If the variable **species** isn't assigned "cat," then of course it's *not* "cat." So there's no reason to test for *not* "cat." The following code is more concise, less goofy, and more readable.

```
1 if species == "cat":
2   print("Yep, it's cat.")
3 else:
4   print("Nope, not cat.")
```

If the test passes—if the string "cat" has been assigned to the variable **species**—the first message displays. If the test fails—if the string "cat" hasn't been assigned to the variable **species**—the second message displays.

Things to notice:

- The keyword **else** gets its own line and a colon at the end.
- Statements that execute in the **else** case are indented.
- As in the **if** case, any number of statements can execute in the **else** case.

Finally, there's **elif**. It's short for *else if*. If no test has been successful yet, an **elif** tries something else.

```
1 if donut_condition == "fresh":
2    buy_score = 10
3 elif donut_price == "low":
4    buy_score = 5
5 else:
6    buy_score = 0
```

In the example above, if donuts are fresh, the score is 10, and Python stops testing. If they aren't fresh (**elif**), Python takes the next step, testing for a low price. If the test passes, the score is 5. If that test too fails (**else**), the score is 0.

You can have any number of **elif** statements. Each one tries a new test when all the tests above it have failed. If any **elif** test succeeds, Python executes any statements tied to it, and skips any tests that come afterward.

Since an **else** statement is a catchall, you would never have more than one of them. It always comes last, stipulating what happens if all tests have failed.

In the example above, we're looking for only one test to pass. If donuts are fresh, we don't do a second test, for price. The **elif** code runs only if the first test fails. But sometimes you don't want to stop testing after one test passes. Then you stick with **if**…

```
1 buy_score = 0
2 if donut_condition == "fresh":
3    buy_score += 10
4 if donut_filling == "chocolate":
5    buy_score += 5
6 if donut_price == "reasonable":
7    buy_score += 7
```

The code assigns an intial value of 0 to the variable **buy_score**. Then it makes three tests. Each test that passes increases the value of **buy_score**. If no test passes, **buy_score** keeps its original value, 0.

Find the interactive coding exercises for this chapter at http://www.ASmarterWayToLearn.com/python/11.html

12
Testing sets of conditions

Using the *if* statement, you've learned to test for a condition. If the condition is met, one or more statements execute. But suppose not one but two conditions have to be met in order for a test to succeed.

For example, if a guy weighs more than 300 pounds, he's just a great big guy. But if he weighs more than 300 pounds *and* runs 40 yards in under 6 seconds? You're going to invite him to try out for the team. You can test for a combination of conditions in Python by using the keyword **and**.

```
1 if weight > 300 and time < 6:
2   status = "try to recruit him"
```

The individual needs to meet both conditions—over 300 pounds and under 6 seconds—in order to qualify. If he meets only one of the conditions, the test fails, and he doesn't get the invitation.

You can chain any number of conditions together.

```
1 if weight > 300 and time < 6 and age > 17 and height >
72:
2   status = "try to recruit him"
```

You can also create a test that passes if *any* condition is met. The keyword is **or**.

```
1 if SAT > avg or GPA > 2.5 or parent == "alum":
2   message = "Welcome to Leeds College!"
```

Only one of the conditions needs to be met in order for the welcome message to be sent out—a high SAT score, a decent grade point average, or a parent who attended the college. Any of them will do. Of course, line 2 executes if more than one condition is met.

You can combine any number of **and** and **or** conditions. When you do, you create ambiguities. Take this line...

```
if age > 65 or age < 21 and res == "U.K.":
```

This can be read in either of two ways.

The first way it can be read: If the person is over 65 *or* under 21 *and*, in addition to either of these conditions, is also a resident of the U.K. Under this interpretation, both columns in the following table need to be true in order for the overall *if* statement to be true..

Over 65 or under 21	Resident of U.K.

The second way it can be read: If the person is over 65 *and* living anywhere *or* is under 21 *and* a resident of the U.K. Under this interpretation, if either column in the following table is true, the overall *if* statement is true.

Over 65	Under 21 and U.K. resident

It's the same problem you face when you combine mathematical expressions. And you solve it the same way: with parentheses.

In the following code, if the subject is over 65 *and* a U.K. resident, it's a pass. Or, if the subject is under 21 *and* a U.K. resident, it's a pass.

```
if (age > 65 or age < 21) and res == "U.K.":
```

In the following code, if the subject is over 65 *and* living anywhere, the overall *if* statement is true. Or, if the subject is under 21 *and* living in the U.K., it's a pass.

```
if age > 65 or (age < 21 and res == "U.K."):
```

Find the interactive coding exercises for this chapter at
http://www.ASmarterWayToLearn.com/python/12.html

13
if statements nested

Check out this code.

```
1 if (x == y or a == b) and c == d:
2    g = h
3 else:
4    e = f
```

In the code above, if either of the first conditions is true—**x** has the same value as **y** or **a** has the same value as **b**— and, in addition, the third condition is true—**c** has the same value as **d**—then **g** is assigned the value of **h**. Otherwise, **e** is assigned the value of **f**.

There's another way to code this, using nesting.

```
1 if c == d:
2    if x == y:
3       g = h
4    elif a == b:
5       g = h
6    else:
7       e = f
8 else:
9    e = f
```

Nest levels are communicated to Python by indentations. There are three second-level blocks nested inside the top-level **if**.

```
1 if c == d:
2    if x == y:
3       g = h
4    elif a == b:
5       g = h
6    else:
7       e = f
8 else:
9    e = f
```

The un-nested first-level blocks begin with no indentation…

```
1 if c == d:
2    if x == y:
3        g = h
4    elif a == b:
5        g = h
6    else:
7        e = f
8 else:
9    e = f
```

If the condition tested by the top first-level **if**—that **c** has the same value as **d**—is true...

```
1 if c == d:
2    if x == y:
3        g = h
4    elif a == b:
5        g = h
6    else:
7        e = f
8 else:
9    e = f
```

...the three second-level blocks determine what happens...

```
1 if c == d:
2    if x == y:
3        g = h
4    elif a == b:
5        g = h
6    else:
7        e = f
8 else:
9    e = f
```

If the condition tested by the top first-level **if**—that **c** has the same value as **d**—is false...

```
1 if c == d:
2    if x == y:
3       g = h
4    elif a == b:
5       g = h
6    else:
7       e = f
8 else:
9    e = f
```

...the three second-level blocks are skipped...

```
1 if c == d:
2    if x == y:
3       g = h
4    elif a == b:
5       g = h
6    else:
7       e = f
8 else:
9    e = f
```

...and the second first-level block determines what happens...

```
1 if c == d:
2    if x == y:
3       g = h
4    elif a == b:
5       g = h
6    else:
7       e = f
8 else:
9    e = f
```

In the relatively simple set of tests and outcomes shown in this example, I would prefer to use the more concise structure using **and** and **or** that you learned in the last chapter. But when things get really complicated, nested **if**s can be a good way to go.

Find the interactive coding exercises for this chapter at http://www.ASmarterWayToLearn.com/python/13.html

14
Comments

Comments are lines of text in your code that Python ignores.

Comments are for the human, not the machine. For example, a comment can explain a section of code so another programmer can understand it. A comment can help you figure out your code when you come back to it a month or a year later.

```
1 # This is a comment.
2 # This is another comment.
3 # Python ignores these comments.
4 # The code that Python executes is next, on line 5.
5 print("Hello, world!")
```

To write a comment, begin with **#**. For readability, add a space after the **#**.

In addition to helping you and others understand your code later on, comments can help you test and debug. You can use them to *comment out* portions of your code and see what happens.

For example, suppose you have some code that doesn't run:

```
1 if first_name == "Harry":
2   if last_name == "Potter":
3     if interest == "wizardry"
4       print("Welcome back to Hogwarts, Harry!")
```

You suspect the problem might be line 3, so you comment it out and see what happens:

```
1 if first_name == "Harry":
2   if last_name == "Potter":
3     # if interest == "wizardry"
4       print("Welcome back to Hogwarts, Harry!")
```

You try running the code again, with line 3 disabled. And it works!

So you look closely at line 3 and see that it's missing a colon at the end. You add the colon…

```
1 if first_name == "Harry":
2   if last_name == "Potter":
3     if interest == "wizardry":
4       print("Welcome back to Hogwarts, Harry!")
```

…and run the code again. And it works!

In the example we started with, I commented entire lines:

```
1 # This is a comment.
2 # This is another comment.
3 # Python ignores these comments.
4 # The code that Python executes is next, on line 5.
5 print("Hello, world!")
```

You can also place comments to the right of working code:

```
print("Hello, world!") # Greet the world
```

In the code above, Python displays the message and ignores the comment.

If you want to write a multi-line comment, there's an alternative to starting each line with #. You can enclose all the comment lines in three single quotation marks:

```
1 '''
2 This is a comment.
3 This is another comment.
4 Python ignores these comments.
5 The code that Python executes is on line 7.
6 '''
7 print("Hello, world!")
```

Find the interactive coding exercises for this chapter at http://www.ASmarterWayToLearn.com/python/14.html

15
Lists

Let's assign some string values to some variables.

```
city_0 = "Atlanta"
city_1 = "Baltimore"
city_2 = "Chicago"
city_3 = "Denver"
city_4 = "Los Angeles"
city_5 = "Seattle"
```

The variable names are all the same, except they end in different numbers. I could have given the six variables completely different names if I'd wanted to—**a**, **b**, **c**, **d**, **y**, and **z** or **fee**, **fi**, **fo**, **fum**, **foo**, and **oof**—if I'd wanted to, but I chose to name them this particular way because of where this discussion is going.

Now, having made these assignments, if I code...

```
print("Welcome to " + city_3)
```

...Python displays **Welcome to Denver**

I'm going to show you another type of variable, one that will come in handy for many tasks that you'll learn about in later chapters. I'm talking about a type of variable called a *list*. Whereas an ordinary variable has a single value assigned to it—for example **city_2** has a value of "Denver" and *only* "Denver"—a list is a variable that can have a sequence of values assigned to it. In a list, these values are known as *elements*.

You define a list this way:

```
cities = ["Atlanta", "Baltimore", "Chicago", "Denver", "Los
Angeles", "Seattle"]
```

The definition of a list begins the same way the definition of any variable begins—in this case, **cities =**

But when you're defining a list, you enclose everything to the right of the equal sign in square brackets:

```
cities = ["Atlanta", "Baltimore", "Chicago", "Denver", "Los
Angeles", "Seattle"]
```

Each element is separated by a comma and a space:

```
cities = ["Atlanta", "Baltimore", "Chicago", "Denver", "Los
Angeles", "Seattle"]
```

In the example at the beginning of this chapter, I ended each variable name with a number. `city_0` was "Atlanta", `city_1` was "Baltimore", and so on. The list I just defined is similar, but in the case of a list, Python numbers the different elements automatically. And you refer to each element by writing the list name—`cities` in this case—followed by a number enclosed in square brackets. In the list `cities` defined above, `cities[0]` is "Atlanta", `cities[1]` is "Baltimore", and so on.

The first element in a list always has an *index* of 0, the second element an index of 1, and so on.

The following code is like the original statement I coded using the simple variable `city_3`, but now I specify a list element instead of a simple variable:

```
print("Welcome to " + cities[3])
```

Since Denver is the fourth element in the list (remember, the numbering starts at 0, so the fourth element has an index of 3), Python displays **Welcome to Denver**.

A list element can be assigned any type of value that you can assign to ordinary variables, for example a string or a number. You can even mix the different types of values in the same list (not that you would ordinarily want to).

```
mixed_things = [1, "Bob", "Now is"]
```

In the example above, `mixed_things[0]` has a numerical value of 1, `mixed_things[1]` has a value of "Bob", and `mixed_things[2]` has a value of "Now is".

Things to keep in mind:

- The first element in a list always has an index of 0, not 1. This means that if the last element in the list has an index of 9, there are 10 items in the list.

- The same naming rules you learned for ordinary variables apply. Only letters, numbers, and underscores are legal. The first character can't be a number. No spaces.

- It's a good idea to make list names plural—**cities** instead of **city**, for example—since a list usually contains multiple things.

Find the interactive coding exercises for this chapter at
http://www.ASmarterWayToLearn.com/python/15.html

16
Lists: Adding and changing elements

In the last chapter, I declared this list:

```
cities = ["Atlanta", "Baltimore", "Chicago", "Denver", "Los
Angeles", "Seattle"]
```

The list contains six elements, "Atlanta"—**cities[0]**—through "Seattle"—**cities[5]**. Suppose you want to add a seventh city, New York, for example. This is the code:

```
cities.append("New York")
```

The code above tacks on the element "New York" to the end of the list. The list now has seven elements. **cities[6]** has a value of "New York".

The statement begins with the list name:

```
cities.append("New York")
```

Next there's a dot:

```
cities.append("New York")
```

Then the keyword **append**:

```
cities.append("New York")
```

The value, in this case the string "New York," is enclosed in parentheses:

```
cities.append("New York")
```

If you're adding a number instead of a string, you don't enclose the number in quotation marks:

```
scores.append(47)
```

There's an alternative way to append. It allows you to add one or more elements to a list. The following code adds two new elements, "Dubuque" and "New Orleans," to the **cities** list:

```
cities = cities + ["Dubuque", "New Orleans"]
```

You can use the same syntax to create a second list by adding on to an existing list.

```
longer_list_of_cities = cities + ["Dubuque", "New Orleans"]
```

You can create an empty list using square brackets with nothing in them...

```
todays_tasks = []
```

...then later add elements so the list is no longer empty...

```
todays_tasks = todays_tasks + ["Walk dog", "Buy groceries"]
```

Instead of appending an element to the end of a list, you can insert it into the list where you want it. This is the **cities** list as I originally defined it:

cities[0] is "Atlanta"
cities[1] is "Baltimore"
cities[2] is "Chicago"
cities[3] is "Denver"
cities[4] is "Los Angeles"
cities[5] is "Seattle"

If I want to insert "New York" at the beginning of the list, I write...

```
cities.insert(0, "New York")
```

Now "New York" has an index of 0. It's at the beginning of the list, and all the other elements have moved down the list to make room for "New York":

cities[0] is "New York"
cities[1] is "Atlanta"
cities[2] is "Baltimore"
cities[3] is "Chicago"
cities[4] is "Denver"
cities[5] is "Los Angeles"
cities[6] is "Seattle"

As in the **append** statement, the **insert** statement begins with the list name, followed by a dot:

```
cities.insert(0, "New York")
```

Then comes the keyword:

```
cities.insert(0, "New York")
```

The rest of it is enclosed in parentheses:

```
cities.insert(0, "New York")
```

But this time, there are two things to specify…the index that tells Python where you want the element placed…

```
cities.insert(0, "New York")
```

…and, following a comma and space, the value of the element…

```
cities.insert(0, "New York")
```

Let's say you want to insert "Dallas" before "Baltimore". The index of "Baltimore" is 2. You're going to take that index away from "Baltimore" and give it to "Dallas"…

```
cities.insert(2, "Dallas")
```

"Baltimore" was the element with an index of 2. Now "Dallas" has it. "Baltimore" and all the elements below it move down the list:

```
cities[0] is "New York"
cities[1] is "Atlanta"
cities[2] is "Dallas"
cities[3] is "Baltimore"
cities[4] is "Chicago"
cities[5] is "Denver"
cities[6] is "Los Angeles"
cities[7] is "Seattle"
```

Here's how to assign a new value to an element.
cities[2] is "Dallas." You want to change it to "Houston." This

is the code:

```
cities[2] = "Houston"
```

Find the interactive coding exercises for this chapter at
http://www.ASmarterWayToLearn.com/python/16.html

17
Lists: Taking slices out of them

You can copy consecutive elements of a list to build another list. For example, if you have this list…

```
cities = ["Atlanta", "Baltimore", "Chicago", "Denver", "Los
Angeles", "Seattle"]
```

…you can copy elements 2 through 4 to create another list…

```
smaller_list_of_cities = cities[2:5]
```

…and you wind up with a list named **smaller_list_of_cities** that comprises "Chicago," "Denver," and "Los Angeles."

When you slice from a list, the list is unchanged. Think "copy," not "cut."

Things to note:

The first number inside the brackets targets the first element in the slice:

```
smaller_list_of_cities = cities[2:5]
```

Then comes a colon:

```
smaller_list_of_cities = cities[2:5]
```

The number following the colon is the index number of the element that comes *after* the last element in the slice:

```
smaller_list_of_cities = cities[2:5]
```

So if you want the last element to be the one with an index of 4, that second number has to be 5.

When the first element of the slice is the first element of the original list—the element with an index of 0—you can omit the first number altogether:

```
smaller_list_of_cities = cities[:5]
```

Now **smaller_list_of_cities** comprises "Atlanta,"

"Baltimore," "Chicago," "Denver," and "Los Angeles."

When the last element of the slice is the last element of the original list, you can omit the second number:

```
smaller_list_of_cities = cities[2:]
```

Now **smaller_list_of_cities** comprises "Chicago," "Denver," "Los Angeles," and "Seattle."

Find the interactive coding exercises for this chapter at http://www.ASmarterWayToLearn.com/python/17.html

18
Lists: Deleting and removing elements

Suppose you have a list of things to do:

```
tasks = ["email Frank", "call Sarah", "meet with Zach"]
```

tasks[0] is "email Frank"
tasks[1] is "call Sarah"
tasks[2] is "meet with Zach"

Working through the list from top to bottom, you complete "email Frank", the first of the **tasks**. To strike that element off the list, you write:

```
del tasks[0]
```

Now the list has just two remaining elements:

tasks[0] is "call Sarah"
tasks[1] is "meet with Zach"

Notice that when you delete the original **tasks[0]**, "email Frank," Python adjusts the index numbers so there are no gaps. The new list begins with **tasks[0]**. There is now no **tasks[2]**.

You can delete any list element by specifying its index number. If the original list is...

tasks[0] is "email Frank"
tasks[1] is "call Sarah"
tasks[2] is "meet with Zach"

...to delete "call Sarah", you write:

```
del tasks[1]
```

Again the list has just two remaining elements:

`tasks[0]` is "email Frank"
`tasks[1]` is "meet with Zach"

And again, Python adjusts the index numbers so there are no gaps. The new list begins with **`tasks[0]`**. There is now no **`tasks[2]`**.

Let's go over the syntax:

The statement begins with the keyword **`del`**, short for *delete*:

```
del tasks[1]
```

Next comes a space:

```
del tasks[1]
```

Then the usual way you specify the list element:

```
del tasks[1]
```

You can also strike an element off a list by specifying its value instead of its index number:

```
tasks.remove("call Sarah")
```

Again, the two remaining elements are:

`tasks[0]` is "email Frank"
`tasks[1]` is "meet with Zach"

This operation begins with the list name:

```
tasks.remove("call Sarah")
```

Next, a dot:

```
tasks.remove("call Sarah")
```

Then the keyword **`remove`**:

```
tasks.remove("call Sarah")
```

The value is enclosed in parentheses:

```
tasks.remove("call Sarah")
```

Find the interactive coding exercises for this chapter at

http://www.ASmarterWayToLearn.com/python/18.html

19
Lists: popping elements

When you delete or remove a list element as I showed you in the last chapter, that element disappears into oblivion. It's just gone. But sometimes, you want to strike an element off a list but hang onto it for another purpose. For example, you want to add the element to another list.

Again, here is the list of things to do:

```
tasks = ["email Frank", "call Sarah", "meet with Zach"]
```

tasks[0] is "email Frank"
tasks[1] is "call Sarah"
tasks[2] is "meet with Zach"

After calling Sarah, you want to strike the element off the **tasks** list and add it to the **tasks_accomplished** list. You begin by popping the element into a variable:

```
latest_task_accomplished = tasks.pop(1)
```

Now the **tasks** list has been shortened to…

tasks[0] is "email Frank"
tasks[1] is "meet with Zach"

…and the value of **latest_task_accomplished** is "call Sarah."
Now you can use the variable **latest_task_accomplished** to append "call Sarah" to the list **tasks_accomplished**:

```
tasks_accomplished.append(latest_task_accomplished)
```

Let's go over the syntax.

```
latest_task_accomplished = tasks.pop(1)
```

It begins with the variable that's going to hold the value that's being popped off:

```
latest_task_accomplished = tasks.pop(1)
```

Then comes the equal sign that assigns the value to the variable:

```
latest_task_accomplished = tasks.pop(1)
```

Next, the name of the list:

```
latest_task_accomplished = tasks.pop(1)
```

...a dot...

```
latest_task_accomplished = tasks.pop(1)
```

...the keyword...

```
latest_task_accomplished = tasks.pop(1)
```

...and the index of the targeted element in parentheses:

```
latest_task_accomplished = tasks.pop(1)
```

By combining code segments you already know, you can pop an element off a list and append it to another list:

```
tasks_accomplished.append(tasks.pop(1))
```

The code above strikes the second element off the **tasks** list and adds it to the end of the **tasks_accomplished** list.

By combining code segments you already know, you can pop an element off a list and insert it into another list:

```
tasks_accomplished.insert(1, tasks.pop(1))
```

The code above strikes the second element off the **tasks** list and inserts it as the second element in the **tasks_accomplished** list.

A time-saver: To pop the last element in a list, skip the index number. Leave the parentheses empty. Write:

```
latest_task_accomplished = tasks.pop()
```

Find the interactive coding exercises for this chapter at
http://www.ASmarterWayToLearn.com/python/19.html

20
Tuples

A *tuple*—pronounced "toople" by some people and "tupple" by others—is like a list, but the elements are fixed. They can't be changed—unless you redefine the whole tuple.

Let's say you want to put together a collection of U.S. states in the order in which they were founded. If we limit the elements to the first four states to keep things simple, it would be, in their order of founding...

Delaware
Pennsylvania
New Jersey
Georgia

We're confident these will always be the first four states, and their order won't change. We'll never need to replace one of them with another state. We'll never need to add another state. And, barring extraordinary events, we'll never need to delete one of them. So we create a tuple—a list that's written in stone.

You code a tuple as you would a list, with one exception:

```
states_in_order_of_founding = ("Delaware", "Pennsylvania",
"New Jersey", "Georgia")
```

Do you see the one way a tuple definition is different from a list definition? You use parentheses instead of square brackets.

You pick a particular element out of a tuple the same way you pick an element out of a list:

```
1 second_state_founded = states_in_order_of_founding[1]
2 print("The second state founded was " +
second_state_founded)
```

Like a list, a tuple starts numbering at 0, so
states_in_order_of_founding[1] is second in the series. It's "Pennsylvania". That's the string assigned to

`second_state_founded`.
Python displays:

The second state founded was Pennsylvania

As I said, a tuple doesn't allow you to make any changes in any of the ways that a list allows. You can't add, modify, remove, delete, or pop. If you *must* make a change, you have to define the tuple all over again. For example, suppose Pennsylvanians vote to change the name of their state to Taylorswiftsylvania. You've got to recode the whole tuple:

```
states_in_order_of_founding = ("Delaware",
"Taylorswiftsylvania formerly known as Pennsylvania", "New
Jersey", "Georgia")
```

If the order of elements changes for any reason, you have to re-code the whole tuple, too.

Find the interactive coding exercises for this chapter at http://www.ASmarterWayToLearn.com/python/20.html

21
for loops

Suppose you want to check if a particular city is one of the 5 environmentally cleanest in the U.S.

You've assigned the name of the city in question to the variable **city_to_check**. For example, you wrote…

```
city_to_check = "Tucson"
```

And you've assigned the names of the 5 cleanest cities to the list **cleanest_cities**.

```
cleanest_cities = ["Cheyenne", "Santa Fe", "Tucson", "Great
Falls", "Honolulu"]
```

Now you go through the list to see if the city in question is on the list. If it is, you display the good news.

This is one way to do it:

```
1   if city_to_check == cleanest_cities[0]:
2     print("It's one of the cleanest cities")
3   elif city_to_check == cleanest_cities[1]:
4     print("It's one of the cleanest cities")
5   elif city_to_check == cleanest_cities[2]:
6     print("It's one of the cleanest cities")
7   elif city_to_check == cleanest_cities[3]:
8    print("It's one of the cleanest cities")
9   elif city_to_check == cleanest_cities[4]:
10    print("It's one of the cleanest cities")
```

That's a load of code.

Conveniently, Python provides a more concise approach. It's called a *for* loop. It begins with the keyword **for** and it loops through the same steps again and again:

```
1 for a_clean_city in cleanest_cities:
2   if city_to_check == a_clean_city:
3     print("It's one of the cleanest cities")
```

The code above pulls up each element in the list

cleanest_cities, one by one. With each iteration through the loop, it temporarily assigns the current element in the list to the variable **a_clean_city**. It then checks this value against the value of the variable **city_to_check**.

If Tucson is the city we're asking about, the string "Tucson" has been assigned to **city_to_check**.

The *for* loop starts with the first element in the list. It asks, Is this first element in the **cleanest_cities** list, "Cheyenne," equal to the city we're checking, "Tucson"? No?

Then the loop moves to the second element in the list, Santa Fe. It repeats the same question: Is this second element in the **cleanest_cities** list, "Santa Fe," equal to "Tucson?" No?

The loop tries once again, moving to the third element in the list. It asks, Is this third element in the **cleanest_cities** list, "Tucson," equal to "Tucson"? Yes!

It displays the message "It's one of the cleanest cities."

There are three variables involved in this code. They are the ordinary variables **a_clean_city** and **city_to_check**, and the list (a type of variable) **cleanest_cities**.

With each iteration, the loop assigns a different list element, in this case "Cheyenne" on pass 1, "Santa Fe" on pass 2, etc., to the variable **a_clean_city**. That variable is then compared with **city_to_check**.

Of course, you could use any variable names you like. Python would be happy with the following code, though humans might find it hard to read:

```
1 for x in y:
2   if x == z:
3     print("It's one of the cleanest cities")
```

In the first line, the variable that comes after **for** keeps track of the value of the particular element being tested in each iteration. The name of the list that contains all the elements follows **in**.

In plain English…

```
1 for each element, one at a time, in the list:
2   do something with that element
```

In this case, what we're doing with each element is testing it against the variable whose value has been assigned to **city_to_check**, "Tucson."

Here it is again:

```
1 for a_clean_city in cleanest_cities:
2   if city_to_check == a_clean_city:
3     print("It's one of the cleanest cities")
```

Things to notice:

- Line 1 ends in a colon.

- Line 2 is indented, because it takes its orders from Line 1.

- Line 3 has a deeper indent than Line 2, because it takes its orders from Line 2.

In the course of comparing the city in question against the list of clean cities, if Python finds a match, there's no point in continuing the loop. So you stop the loop by adding a **break** statement:

```
1 for a_clean_city in cleanest_cities:
2   if city_to_check == a_clean_city:
3     print("It's one of the cleanest cities")
4     break
```

Find the interactive coding exercises for this chapter at:
http://www.ASmarterWayToLearn.com/python/21.html

22
for loops nested

Atlantic Records has hired you and me to generate a list of names for future rap stars. To make things easy, we'll start by making separate lists of some first names and last names.

First Names	Last Names
BlueRay	Zzz
Upchuck	Burp
Lojack	Dogbone
Gizmo	Droop
Do-Rag	

By combining each of the first names with each of the last names, we can generate 20 different full names for rappers.

Starting with "BlueRay," we go through the list of last names, generating...

BlueRay Zzz
BlueRay Burp
BlueRay Dogbone
BlueRay Droop

We move to the next first name, "Upchuck." Again, we go through the list of last names, generating...

Upchuck Zzz
Upchuck Burp
Upchuck Dogbone
Upchuck Droop

And so on, combining each first name with each last name.

But look, why not have Python do the repetitive work? We'll use nested *for* statements.

```
1   first_names = ["BlueRay ", "Upchuck ", "Lojack ", "Gizmo
", "Do-Rag "]
2   last_names = ["Zzz", "Burp", "Dogbone", "Droop"]
3   full_names = []
5   for a_first_name in first_names:
6       for a_last_name in last_names:
7           full_names.append(a_first_name + " " + a_last_name)
```

This is how it works:

The second, or inner, loop runs a complete cycle of iterations on each iteration of the first, or outer, loop. The outer loop begins with the first name, BlueRay. The inner loop then runs four iterations, combining BlueRay with each of the four last names—Zzz, Burp, etc. It appends each combination to the list **full_names**. When that's finished, the program returns to the outer loop, which moves to the next first name, Upchuck. Then it jumps to the inner loop, which combines this name with each of the four last names and appends these combinations to the list **full_names**. It keeps going like this until all 20 combinations have been added to the list of full names.

You can have as many levels of nesting as you like.

Each nested loop is indented beyond its outer loop.

Find the interactive coding exercises for this chapter at http://www.ASmarterWayToLearn.com/python/22.html

23
Getting information from the user and converting strings and numbers

Okay, we have a list of America's five environmentally cleanest cities. The user wants to know if her city is on that list. She needs a way to tell us the name of the city she wants us to check. That's what Python's **input** function is for.

Here's the code:

```
city_to_check = input("Enter the name of a city: ")
```

When the code above runs, the message **Enter the name of a city:** displays on the user's screen. Python then waits for the user to type a city name and press **Enter**. The name typed by the user is assigned to the variable **city_to_check**. Then we can run the loop from the last chapter to give the user an answer.

Let's break down the code.

It begins with the variable that's going to store the user's input. The name of the variable is up to you.

```
city_to_check = input("Enter the name of a city: ")
```

The equal sign says, "Assign the user's input, whatever it is, to the variable **city_to_check**."

```
city_to_check = input("Enter the name of a city: ")
```

Next comes the keyword **input**.

```
city_to_check = input("Enter the name of a city: ")
```

The message to be displayed on the user's screen—the *prompt*— is enclosed in parentheses and quotation marks.

```
city_to_check = input("Enter the name of a city: ")
```

Note that you *must* provide a variable to hold the user's input. If you omit it…

```
city_to_check = input("Enter the name of a city: ")
```

…Python breaks.

Python treats the value typed by the user as a string, even if it's a number. For example, if you write…

```
monthly_income = input("Enter your monthly income: ")
```

…and the user enters 4000…

…and you try to multiply it by 12 to calculate the user's annual income…

…Python breaks.

That's because you've asked Python to multiply something that Python considers a string—"4000" not 4000—so multiplication is impossible.

If you want it to be a number that Python can do math on, you must convert it.

To convert the string to an integer, write…

```
monthly_income_as_an_integer = int(monthly_income)
```

monthly_income_as_an_integer is, as I think you know by now, a variable name I made up. You can use any other legal variable name instead.

int is a keyword that's short for integer.

To convert a string to a float—a number with decimal places—use the keyword **float**:

```
monthly_income_as_a_float = float(monthly_income)
```

Sometimes you need to convert a number to a string. For example, suppose Python has looked up the minimum wage in your state. It's 15, a number. It's stored in the variable **min_wage**. If you write…

```
print("The minimum wage in your state is $" + min_wage)
```

…Python breaks, because you've asked it to concatenate a string with a number, which it can't do. So you convert the number to a string:

```
min_wage = str(min_wage)
```

Find the interactive coding exercises for this chapter at
http://www.ASmarterWayToLearn.com/python/23.html

24
Changing case

Using **input**, you ask the user to enter her city. Then you check her city against a list of the 5 cleanest cities.

If the user enters "Cheyenne" or any of the other cleanest cities, your code displays a message telling her that it's one of the cleanest cities.

But what if she enters "cheyenne" instead of "Cheyenne"—as some users inevitably will? When that happens, there will be no match. Python is literal-minded. To Python, "cheyenne" is not "Cheyenne."

A human knows that in this context "cheyenne" means "Cheyenne." But Python doesn't. We need some way to get Python to recognize the uncapitalized version as a match.

One way would be to expand the **cleanest_cities** list to include the uncapitalized versions of all the city names:

```
cleanest_cities = ["Cheyenne", "cheyenne", "Santa Fe",
"santa fe", "Tucson", "tucson", "Great Falls", "great
falls", "Honolulu", "honolulu"]
```

That's a lot of extra coding. Plus, if the user enters "santa Fe," "Santa fe," or "sAnta Fe," we're back to the original problem. To cover all these possibilities and others, it would take a mile of code.

The solution is to code the list elements in lowercase, and convert the user's input, whatever it is, to lowercase as well, so we always have apples to compare with apples.

```
1 city_to_check = input("Enter your city: ")
2 city_to_check = city_to_check.lower()
3 cleanest_cities = ["cheyenne", "santa fe", "tucson",
"great falls", "honolulu"]
4 for a_clean_city in cleanest_cities:
5   if city_to_check == a_clean_city:
6     print("It's one of the cleanest cities")
```

Line 2 coverts the user's input to all-lowercase.

Line 3 assigns the names of the cleanest cities—in all-lowercase—to the list **cleanest_cities**. So now we can be sure we're comparing apples to apples.

The conversion code begins with the variable for storing the converted string:

```
2 city_to_check = city_to_check.lower()
```

I chose to use the same variable that I had used to store the user's entry, **city_to_check**. If I wanted to preserve the user's entry, I could use a different variable for the converted string, for example…

```
2 lowercase_city_to_check = city_to_check.lower()
```

The equal sign says, "Assign the result of the conversion that follows to the variable that precedes me."

```
2 city_to_check = city_to_check.lower()
```

Next comes the variable where the user's entry is stored:

```
2 city_to_check = city_to_check.lower()
```

Finally, the conversion function—a dot, and the keyword **lower** followed by empty parentheses.

```
2 city_to_check = city_to_check.lower()
```

You could go the other way and convert the user's entry to all-uppercase, then test against "CHEYENNE," "SANTA FE, " etc. Most coders prefer the lowercase approach. But to convert the string to all-uppercase, you'd write:

```
2 city_to_check = city_to_check.upper()
```

But suppose you've converted the user's input to all-lowercase, and now you want to display a message using **city_to_check**. For example:

```
print("Great news! " + city_to_check + " is one of the
cleanest cities.")
```

Suppose you've converted the string stored in **city_to_check** to all-lowercase for comparison with each lowercase list element. Now you want to use the variable to display a message to the user. But this will produce a result you don't want: the city name in all-lowercase: **Great News! cheyenne is one of the cleanest cities.**

So you do another conversion to give the city name an initial capital letter:

```
city_to_check = city_to_check.title()
```

The **title** function converts "cheyenne" to "Chyenne" and "santa fe" to "Santa Fe."

Find the interactive coding exercises for this chapter at http://www.ASmarterWayToLearn.com/python/24.html

25
Dictionaries: What they are

Earlier in the book you learned to create a list:

```
my_cats = ["Draco", "Bellatrix", "Voldemort"]
```

To pick an element out of the list, you specify an index number:

```
print(my_cats[0])
```

The code above displays **Draco**, the first element in the list, the one with an index of 0.

Lists are good when you're putting together a simple series of things—tasks to do, cooking ingredients, the names of environmentally clean cities.

But sometimes you want to put together something more complicated. For example:

Customer 29876's first name: David
Customer 29876's last name: Elliott
Customer 29876's address: 4803 Wellesley St.
Customer 29876's city: Toronto
Customer 29876's province: ON
Customer 29876's country: Canada
Customer 29876's postal code: M7A1N3

When you're working with Customer 29876's information, you want to be able to pick something out of the series by asking, for example, "What's the customer's province?" So you create a *dictionary*.

A dictionary works something like a list, but instead of a simple series of things, a dictionary is a series of *pairs* of things. Each pair contains a *key*—"first name", "last name" etc.—and a *value*—"David", "Elliott", etc.

To pick something out of a dictionary, you specify a particular key and ask what value is paired with it. In other words, if the key is "first name," for example, what is the value? Answer: "David."

In the next chapter, I'll show you how to create a dictionary.

Find the interactive coding exercises for this chapter at
http://www.ASmarterWayToLearn.com/python/25.html

26
Dictionaries: How to code one

In the last chapter you learned that a dictionary is a series of paired keys and values.

Suppose we're creating a dictionary named **customer_29876**, with these pairs:

key is "first name", value is "David"
key is "last name", value is "Elliott"
key is "address", value is "4803 Wellesley St."

This is the code:

```
customer_29876 = {"first name": "David", "last name":
"Elliott", "address": "4803 Wellesley St."}
```

This structure is similar to the code for creating a list.
Both begin with a variable name and equal sign:

```
jobs_to_do_1st = ["email", "texting", "calls"]
```

```
customer_29876 = {"first name": "David", "last name":
"Elliott", "address": "4803 Wellesley St."}
```

Things are separated by commas:

```
jobs_to_do_1st = ["email", "texting", "calls"]
```

```
customer_29876 = {"first name": "David", "last name":
"Elliott", "address": "4803 Wellesley St."}
```

The series is enclosed in brackets—but in a list, brackets are square brackets, and in a dictionary, brackets are curly brackets.

```
jobs_to_do_1st = ["email", "texting", "calls"]
```

```
customer_29876 = {"first name": "David", "last name":
"Elliott", "address": "4803 Wellesley St."}
```

The big difference: In a list, each chunk is one thing. In a dictionary, each chunk is a paired key and value:

```
jobs_to_do_1st = ["email", "texting", "calls"]

customer_29876 = {"first name": "David", "last name":
"Elliott", "address": "4803 Wellesley St."}
```

Notice that the key is followed by a colon:

```
customer_29876 = {"first name": "David", "last name":
"Elliott", "address": "4803 Wellesley St."}
```

Notice also that the variable name is singular, not plural. I told you in an earlier chapter that you'd normally want to make a list name plural, because you wouldn't say "Here's a list of holiday" or "Here's all my pet." But with a dictionary, it often feels right to keep it singular. You *could* call the dictionary something like **customer_29876_details**, but **customer_29876** is shorter.

Finally, notice that in this example, all the values are strings, enclosed in quotation marks, and so are all the keys:

```
customer_29876 = {"first name": "David", "last name":
"Elliott", "address": "4803 Wellesley St."}
```

Neither keys nor values have to be strings. More about that later.

Find the interactive coding exercises for this chapter at
http://www.ASmarterWayToLearn.com/python/26.html

27
Dictionaries: How to pick information out of them

In the last chapter I coded a dictionary named **customer_29876**.

```
customer_29876 = {"first name": "David", "last name":
"Elliott", "address": "4803 Wellesley St."}
```

The dictionary comprises three pairs:

key is "first name", value is "David"
key is "last name", value is "Elliott"
key is "address", value is "4803 Wellesley St."

The purpose of a dictionary is to store information that you can later lay your hands on. For example, you might want to know what David Elliot's address is. How do you find it?

Remember how to find information in a list?

```
city_to_check = cities[3]
```

In a list, you pick out an element by specifying its index. In the code above, the element in the list **city_to_check** that has an index of 3—that would be the fourth element, since the numbering starts at 0—is picked out, then placed into the variable **city_to_check**.

In a dictionary, the code is similar, except that you pick out an element by specifying its key:

```
address_of_customer = customer_29876["address"]
```

In the code above, Python finds the value in the dictionary **customer_29876** that has the key "address" and assigns the string to the variable **address_of_customer**. Now the string "4803 Wellesley St." is stored in the variable **address_of_customer**.

If you write…

```
print(address_of_customer)
```

…Python displays **4803 Wellesley St.**

The key in this case is a string, "address." But as I mentioned in the last chapter, a key doesn't have to be a string. Nor does a value. Let's talk about that next.

Find the interactive coding exercises for this chapter at
http://www.ASmarterWayToLearn.com/python/27.html

28
Dictionaries: The versatility of keys and values

In the dictionary I've been using as an example, **customer_29876**, the keys are strings, enclosed in quotation marks:

```
customer_29876 = {"first name": "David", "last name": "Elliott", "address": "4803 Wellesley St."}
```

The values are strings, too:

```
customer_29876 = {"first name": "David", "last name": "Elliott", "address": "4803 Wellesley St."}
```

But keys don't have to be strings. They can be numbers:

```
rankings = {5: "Finland", 2: "Norway", 3: "Sweden", 7: "Iceland"}
```

In each pair shown above, the key is a number, not enclosed in quotation marks.

To pick out a value, you use the number:

```
second_ranking_country = rankings[2]
```

rankings[2] is "Norway."
Values can be numbers, too:

```
country_ranks_so_far = {"Finland": 5, "Norway": 2, "Sweden": 3, "Iceland": 7}
```

To pick out a value, you use the key, a string in this case:

```
norway_ranking = country_ranks_so_far["Norway"]
```

country_ranks_so_far["Norway"] is 2.
You can mix strings and numbers any way you want.

```
things_to_remember = {0: "the lowest number", "a dozen": 12, "snake eyes": "a pair of ones", 13: "a baker's dozen"}
```

These are the pairs:

key is the number 0, value is the string "the lowest number"
key is the string "a dozen", value is the number 12
key is the string "snake eyes", value is the string "a pair of ones"
key is the number 13, value is the string "a baker's dozen"

When you're defining a dictionary that contains more than two or three key-value pairs, it's a good idea to break the pairs into separate lines for readability:

```
1 things_to_remember = {
2   0: "the lowest number",
3   "a dozen": 12,
4   "snake eyes": "a pair of ones",
5   13: "a baker's dozen",
6 }
```

Things to notice:

- Each pair is indented.

- Though it isn't necessary, I added a comma after the last pair. Python doesn't mind it, and it means I won't get into trouble by forgetting to insert the comma if I add another key-value pair later. From now on, I'll ask you to adopt this convention when you're doing the exercises.

Find the interactive coding exercises for this chapter at http://www.ASmarterWayToLearn.com/python/28.html

29
Dictionaries: Adding items

Remember how to pick something out of a dictionary?

```
address_of_customer = customer_29876["address"]
```

You begin with the name of the dictionary...

```
address_of_customer = customer_29876["address"]
```

...then you write the key, enclosed in square brackets...

```
address_of_customer = customer_29876["address"]
```

...which retrieves the value "4803 Wellesley St." in our example. Let me show you how to add a key-value pair to a dictionary. The dictionary **customer_29876** has these pairs...

key is "first name", value is "David"
key is "last name", value is "Elliott"
key is "address", value is "4803 Wellesley St."

You can add a new pair by writing...

```
customer_29876["city"] = "Toronto"
```

In the code above, you have those familiar pieces—the dictionary name, the key in square brackets, and the value. They're just in a different order.

Now **customer_29876** has these pairs...

key is "first name", value is "David"
key is "last name", value is "Elliott"
key is "address", value is "4803 Wellesley St."
key is "city", value is "Toronto"

Earlier, you learned how to define a dictionary by assigning it key-value pairs:

```
1 things_to_remember = {
2   0: "the lowest number",
3   "a dozen": 12,
4   "snake eyes": "a pair of ones",
5   13: "a baker's dozen",
6 }
```

You can also define an empty dictionary, a dictionary with no key-value pairs:

```
things_to_remember = {}
```

Later, you can fill the dictionary with pairs, adding one at a time:

```
1 things_to_remember[0] = "the lowest number"
2 things_to_remember["a dozen"] = 12
3 ...etc.
```

Find the interactive coding exercises for this chapter at
http://www.ASmarterWayToLearn.com/python/29.html

30
Dictionaries: Removing and changing items

If you remember how to delete an element from a list...

```
del tasks[0]
```

...you may be able to guess how to delete a key-value pair from a dictionary:

```
del customer_29876["address"]
```

It begins with the same keyword:

```
del tasks[0]
del customer_29876["address"]
```

Then comes the name of the list or dictionary:

```
del tasks[0]
del customer_29876["address"]
```

And the particular piece of information you're after is specified by the index (in the list) or the key (in the dictionary), in square brackets:

```
del tasks[0]
del customer_29876["address"]
```

Changing the value of an element is similar to the same operation that you learned for lists. It begins with the name of the list or dictionary:

```
cities[2] = "Houston"
customer_29876["city"] = "Winipeg"
```

Then comes the index (in the list) or the key (in the dictionary), in square brackets:

```
cities[2] = "Houston"
customer_29876["city"] = "Winipeg"
```

Then the assignment of the new value:

```
cities[2] = "Houston"
customer_29876["city"] = "Winipeg"
```

Find the interactive coding exercises for this chapter at
http://www.ASmarterWayToLearn.com/python/30.html

31
Dictionaries: Looping through values

Let's say you want to display all the values in the **customer_29876** dictionary. Using the abbreviated example from earlier chapters, you could write:

```
1 print(customer_29876["first name"])
2 print(customer_29876["last name"])
3 print(customer_29876["address"])
```

Python displays:

David
Elliott
4803 Wellesley St.

This works, but suppose this were a more realistic dictionary containing twenty or thirty pieces of information about David Elliott. We'd all prefer not to write twenty or thirty lines of code to retrieve and display all the values.

To the rescue comes looping.

Recall how you learned to loop through a list. The following code loops through a list named **cleanest_cities** and displays the name of each city:

```
1 for a_clean_city in cleanest_cities:
2   print(a_clean_city)
```

Following the instructions above, Python displays...

Cheyenne
Santa Fe
Tucson
Great Falls
Honolulu

The code for looping through a dictionary is similar.

```
1 for each_value in customer_29876.values():
2    print(each_value)
```

Following the instructions above, Python displays:

David
Elliott
4803 Wellesley St.

Let's break it down.
The loop begins with the familiar **for**:

```
1 for each_value in customer_29876.values():
2    print(each_value)
```

Next comes a variable to store the value for each iteration.

```
1 for each_value in customer_29876.values():
2    print(each_value)
```

Note: **each_value** is a variable. You can give it any legal variable name you like.

Next, the keyword **in** followed by the name of the dictionary, **customer_29876**:

```
1 for each_value in customer_29876.values():
2    print(each_value)
```

Then a dot…

```
1 for each_value in customer_29876.values():
2    print(each_value)
```

Then the keyword **values**…

```
1 for each_value in customer_29876.values():
2    print(each_value)
```

…then empty parentheses…

```
1 for each_value in customer_29876.values():
2    print(each_value)
```

…and a colon…

```
1 for each_value in customer_29876.values():
2    print(each_value)
```

Repeat it to yourself as many times as you need to, to memorize it:
"Dot values parentheses colon."
Got it?
As in a list loop, there's code that tells Python what action(s) to take
each time through the loop. This code is indented:

```
1 for each_value in customer_29876.values():
2    print(each_value)
```

Find the interactive coding exercises for this chapter at
http://www.ASmarterWayToLearn.com/python/31.html

32
Dictionaries: Looping through keys

In the last chapter you learned to loop through a dictionary, capturing all the values in it:

```
1 for each_value in customer_29876.values():
2     print(each_value)
```

There may be times when you want to capture the keys instead. This is the dictionary:

```
customer_29876 = {
  "first name": "David",
  "last name": "Elliott",
  "address": "4803 Wellesley St.",
}
```

This is the loop:

```
1 for each_key in customer_29876.keys():
2     print(each_key)
```

Python displays:

first name
last name
address

From Python's point of view, the only difference is that you write the keyword **keys**...

```
1 for each_key in customer_29876.keys():
2     print(each_key)
```

...instead of the keyword **values**...

```
1 for each_value in customer_29876.values():
2     print(each_value)
```

Python doesn't care how you name variables as long as they're legal, but I made one more change so the code would make sense to humans. I wrote…

```
1 for each_key etc.
```

…instead of…

```
1 for each_value etc.
```

Find the interactive coding exercises for this chapter at http://www.ASmarterWayToLearn.com/python/32.html

33
Dictionaries: Looping through key-value pairs

You've looped through a dictionary finding all its values, and you've looped through a dictionary finding all its keys. Now I'll show you how to loop through a dictionary finding both keys and values.

This is the dictionary we've been working with:

```
1 customer_29876 = {
2   "first name": "David",
3   "last name": "Elliott",
4   "address": "4803 Wellesley St.",
5 }
```

Here's the code for looping through the dictionary and printing all the keys and values:

```
1 for each_key, each_value in customer_29876.items():
2   print("The customer's " + each_key + " is " +
each value)
```

Following the instructions above, Python displays:

The customer's first name is David
The customer's last name is Elliott
The customer's address is 4803 Wellesley St.

This loop looks like the loops you've been coding, with two exceptions.

First, instead of a single variable that comes after the keyword **for**...

```
1 for each_value in customer_29876.values():
2   print(each_value)
```

...you code 2 variables (your choice of names), one for keys and another for values:

```
1 for each_key, each_value in customer_29876.items():
2    print("The customer's " + each_key + " is " +
each_value)
```

Note that a comma and space separate the two variables:

```
1 for each_key, each_value in customer_29876.items():
2    print("The customer's " + each_key + " is " +
each_value)
```

And the keyword that comes before the empty parentheses changes. Now it's **items**..

```
1 for each_key, each_value in customer_29876.items():
2    print("The customer's " + each_key + " is " +
each_value)
```

Find the interactive coding exercises for this chapter at http://www.ASmarterWayToLearn.com/python/33.html

34
Creating a list of dictionaries

We've been working with a dictionary named **customer_29876**. In our simplified example, the dictionary has three key-value pairs:

```
1 customer_29876 = {
2    "first name": "David",
3    "last name": "Elliott",
4    "address": "4803 Wellesley St.",
5 }
```

One would hope that a company has more than one customer. This means you need more than one dictionary. You need one for each customer. In our example, each dictionary represents a single customer and contains his or her first name, last name, and address.

So instead of creating a single dictionary for **customer_29876**, let's create a list of three dictionaries, one for each of three customers.

You already know how to create a list.

```
customer_ids = [101, 102, 103]
```

The code above creates a list of three integers.

Here's the code for creating a list of—not integers, not strings—but a list of dictionaries. The code also creates the dictionaries themselves:

```
1 customers = [
2   {
3     "customer id": 0,
4     "first name":"John",
5     "last name": "Ogden",
6     "address": "301 Arbor Rd.",
7   },
8   {
9     "customer id": 1,
10    "first name":"Ann",
11    "last name": "Sattermyer",
12    "address": "PO Box 1145",
13  },
14  {
15    "customer id": 2,
16    "first name":"Jill",
17    "last name": "Somers",
18    "address": "3 Main St.",
19  },
20 ]
```

Some things about this code are already familiar to you. The code begins with a standard list definition, starting with the list name, **customers**. The name is followed by an equal sign. Then come the three elements of the list, enclosed in square brackets.

What's new is that the three elements are neither strings nor numbers. They're dictionaries.

As in any list, the three elements—the three dictionaries—are enclosed in square brackets.

As in any dictionary, the three key-value pairs in these dictionaries are enclosed in curly brackets and separated by commas.

One more thing that's new: the dictionaries don't have names. There is no **customer_29876**. Each customer does have an identifying number, but the number is no longer part of a dictionary name. Now the customer number is an integer, a value like 101, 102, or 103 that's paired with a key, "customer id."

Note the formatting. The three elements of the list, the dictionaries, are indented. The three items in each dictionary, the key-value pairs, are indented to the second level.

Find the interactive coding exercises for this chapter at http://www.ASmarterWayToLearn.com/python/34.html

35
How to pick information out of a list of dictionaries

You know how to pick information out of a dictionary by specifying the dictionary's name and the key that summons the value you want:

```
customer_first_name = customer_29876["first name"]
```

The code above says, "Look into the dictionary whose name is **customer_29876**. In this dictionary find the value that is paired with the key "first name."

But in our *list* of dictionaries we created in the last chapter, the dictionaries have no name. How do we get any information out of them when we can't specify a dictionary name? How do we tell Python which dictionary to look into to find, for example, a particular customer's address?

In the example, I solved the problem by setting up the customer ids a certain way:

```
customers = [
    {
        "customer id": 0,
        "first name":"John",
        "last name": "Ogden",
        "address": "301 Arbor Rd.",
    },
    {
        "customer id": 1,
        "first name":"Ann",
        "last name": "Sattermyer",
        "address": "PO Box 1145",
    },
    {
        "customer id": 2,
        "first name":"Jill",
        "last name": "Somers",
        "address": "3 Main St.",
    },
]
```

In a list of strings, numbers, dictionaries, or anything else, the first item on the list gets an index of 0, provided automatically by Python. In the example above, John Ogden's information is contained in the first dictionary in the list **customers**. Python assigns this dictionary the index 0. John Ogden's customer id is up to me. I can give him any customer id I want. I choose to match his id to the index of the dictionary. I give him a customer id of 0, the same as the dictionary's index.

The customer whose information is contained in the second dictionary in the list, the dictionary with an index of 1, also gets a matching number—a customer id of 1. The next customer gets an id of 2, etc. So all through the list of dictionaries, the customer id always matches the index of the dictionary.

If I want to know which dictionary John Ogden's information is in, I don't need a dictionary name. All I need is his customer id—0. This tells me where to find his dictionary—at the 0 index in the list.

Let's say I want to know the address of a customer whose id is 2870. This is the code that finds it:

```
1 dictionary_to_look_in = customers[2870]
2 customer_address = dictionary_to_look_in["address"]
```

The code assigns the dictionary whose index number in the **customers** list is 2870…

```
1 dictionary_to_look_in = customers[2870]
2 customer_address = dictionary_to_look_in["address"]
```

…to the variable **dictionary_to_look_in**.

```
1 dictionary_to_look_in = customers[2870]
2 customer_address = dictionary_to_look_in["address"]
```

This variable, **dictionary_to_look_in**, is used in line 2 to find the address of the customer whose id is 2870:

```
1 dictionary_to_look_in = customers[2870]
2 customer_address = dictionary_to_look_in["address"]
```

And the address is assigned to the variable **customer_address**:

```
1 dictionary_to_look_in = customers[2870]
2 customers_address = dictionary_to_look_in["address"]
```

One constraint presented by this scheme: If you lose a customer, you can't delete her dictionary from the list. If you do, index numbers of dictionaries will change. They'll stop matching the customer ids inside them. For example, if you delete the dictionary that has an index of 350 in the list, whose customer id is also 350, the next dictionary, with an original index of 351, will now have an index of 350. The customer's id in that dictionary will still be 351, but the dictionary's position on the list will have moved up to 350. You'll no longer be able to target the dictionary by using the customer id. And the same thing will happen with all the dictionaries that come afterward.

The solution is to keep the original list of dictionaries intact, and create a second list of customers who are no longer active. Then if, for example, you want to mail all active customers, you use the second list to filter inactive customers in the first list out of the mailing list.

Find the interactive coding exercises for this chapter at http://www.ASmarterWayToLearn.com/python/35.html

36
How to append a new dictionary to a list of dictionaries

In the simplified example we're using, the list is named **customers**. Each dictionary in the list contains four key-value pairs that tell us the customer id, first name, last name, and address of that particular customer.

We've acquired a new customer. So we need to add a new dictionary to the end of the list.

Let's say we already have the first name, last name, and address of the new customer. These values are stored in the variables **new_first_name**, **new_last_name**, and **new_address**.

Using the scheme I showed you in the last chapter, we're going to make the customer id match the index of the dictionary.

There's an easy way to find out what that index is going to be.

If we can find out how many dictionaries are already in the list, that number will be the index number of the new dictionary. Remember, the number of dictionaries in the list is 1 greater than the largest index number, since index numbering starts at 0. If the number of dictionaries in the list is 1000, the last dictionary in the list has an index of 999. So the index number of the new dictionary will be 1000.

And if we know what that index number of the new dictionary on the list is, we know what the new customer id is going to be, because it's going to be the same number.

To learn how many dictionaries are in the list, we measure the list's *length*. Using the keyword **len**, for length, we write...

```
new_customer_id = len(customers)
```

If the length of the **customers** list is 1000—if there are 1000 dictionaries in the list—it means the index number of the last dictionary in the list is 999 – 1 since the count of dictionaries in the list starts at 1 and indexing starts at 0. So the new customer id is the list length: 1000. That's the number assigned to the variable **new_customer_id**.

Note how the code is structured:

It's the keyword **len**…

```
new_customer_id = len(customers)
```

…followed by the list name enclosed by parentheses…

```
new_customer_id = len(customers)
```

Now we've got all the values, including the new customer id, loaded into variables. We can create the new dictionary:

```
new_dictionary = {
    "customer id": new_customer_id,
    "first name": new_first_name,
    "last name": new_last_name,
    "address": new_address,
}
```

Finally, we append this new dictionary to the list:

```
customers.append(new_dictionary)
```

Find the interactive coding exercises for this chapter at http://www.ASmarterWayToLearn.com/python/36.html

37
Creating a dictionary that contains lists

Let's return to our favorite customer from an earlier chapter. His information is held in the dictionary named **customer_29876**.

His first name, last name, and address are in three key-value pairs:

```
1 customer_29876 = {
2   "first name": "David",
3   "last name": "Elliott",
4   "address": "4803 Wellesley St.",
5 }
```

Let's say we offer our customers different discounts. David Elliott has qualified for three of them: a standard discount, a volume discount, and a loyalty discount. A good way to include this information in the dictionary is to code the discounts as a list and put the list in the dictionary. This is the code:

```
1 customer_29876 = {
2   "first name": "David",
3   "last name": "Elliott",
4   "address": "4803 Wellesley St.",
5   "discounts": ["standard", "volume", "loyalty"],
6 }
```

Line 5 uses the syntax you already know for creating a list. It's the list name followed by a colon...

```
5   "discounts": ["standard", "volume", "loyalty"],
```

...then the series of values, enclosed in square brackets...

```
5   "discounts": ["standard", "volume", "loyalty"],
```

But the list is created inside the dictionary definition.

And the name of the list, "discounts," is also the dictionary key paired with the value, the series of three strings.

Find the interactive coding exercises for this chapter at
http://www.ASmarterWayToLearn.com/python/37.html

38
How to get information out of a list within a dictionary

customer_29876 qualifies for three discounts, standard, volume, and loyalty. He doesn't qualify for a fourth discount, brother-in-law.

When he makes a purchase, we want to give him the biggest discount he qualifies for, but only that one discount. If we give him all the discounts he qualifies for, we'll lose money.

These are the discounts:

brother-in-law – 30%
loyalty – 15%
volume – 10%
standard – 5%

To find out which discount to give **customer_29876**, we go through the list of discounts named "discounts" in the dictionary **customer_29876**. We look for each discount in turn, starting with the largest one, the brother-in-law discount. When we find a discount, the search stops, and that's the discount we apply.

This code introduces you to a new way to use the keyword **in**:

```
1 if "brother-in-law" in customer_29876["discounts"]:
2   discount_amount = .30
3 elif "loyalty" in customer_29876["discounts"]:
4   discount_amount = .15
5 elif "volume" in customer_29876["discounts"]:
6   discount_amount = .10
7 elif "standard" in customer_29876["discounts"]:
8   discount_amount = .05
```

Since "loyalty" is found in the list within the **customer_29876** dictionary, the 15% discount is applied.

The code above tells Python to check for a string…

```
1 if "brother-in-law" in customer_29876["discounts"]:
2     discount_amount = .30
```

...in...

```
1 if "brother-in-law" in customer_29876["discounts"]:
2     discount_amount = .30
```

...the "discounts" list...

```
1 if "brother-in-law" in customer_29876["discounts"]:
2     discount_amount = .30
```

...within the **customer_29876** dictionary...

```
1 if "brother-in-law" in customer_29876["discounts"]:
2     discount_amount = .30
```

...and if it's in there, assign the correct value to the variable
discount_amount...

```
1 if "brother-in-law" in customer_29876["discounts"]:
2     discount_amount = .30
```

If the string isn't found, check for the next discount...

```
3 elif "loyalty" in customer_29876["discounts"]:
4     discount_amount = .15
```

Find the interactive coding exercises for this chapter at
http://www.ASmarterWayToLearn.com/python/38.html

39
Creating a dictionary that contains a dictionary

When we organized customer information as a list of dictionaries, it worked, but we had to accept a constraint. The customer id, the first value in the dictionary, had to match the index number of the dictionary in the list. That meant we could never delete a customer. Otherwise, we'd throw the whole thing off.

But what if we turned the list of dictionaries into a dictionary of dictionaries? By replacing index numbers with key-value pairs, we wouldn't be locked in to a sequence of numbers that have to remain unbroken. We could delete a customer without wrecking the whole thing.

Here's the list of dictionaries that we coded earlier:

```
1  customers = [
2    {
3      "customer id": 0,
4      "first name":"John",
5      "last name": "Ogden",
6      "address": "301 Arbor Rd.",
7    },
8    {
9      "customer id": 1,
10     "first name":"Ann",
11     "last name": "Sattermyer",
12     "address": "PO Box 1145",
13   },
14   {
15     "customer id": 2,
16     "first name":"Jill",
17     "last name": "Somers",
18     "address": "3 Main St.",
19   },
20 ]
```

In this list, there are three dictionaries. Each dictionary has four key-value pairs. The opening square bracket on line 1 and the closing square bracket on line 20 enclose the list.

Let's begin by replacing the pair of square brackets with a pair of curly brackets:

```
1 customers = {
2    {
3       "customer id": 0,
4       "first name":"John",
5       "last name": "Ogden",
6       "address": "301 Arbor Rd.",
7    },
8    {
9       "customer id": 1,
10      "first name":"Ann",
11      "last name": "Sattermyer",
12      "address": "PO Box 1145",
13   },
14   {
15      "customer id": 2,
16      "first name":"Jill",
17      "last name": "Somers",
18      "address": "3 Main St.",
19   },
20 }
```

By replacing the square brackets with curly brackets, we're saying that **customers** is a dictionary instead of a list. But a dictionary contains key-value pairs. What are the values of this dictionary?

The dictionary has three values—the three inner dictionaries:

```
1 customers = {
2    {
3       "customer id": 0,
4       "first name":"John",
5       "last name": "Ogden",
6       "address": "301 Arbor Rd.",
7    },
8    {
9       "customer id": 1,
10      "first name":"Ann",
11      "last name": "Sattermyer",
12      "address": "PO Box 1145",
13   },
14   {
15      "customer id": 2,
16      "first name":"Jill",
17      "last name": "Somers",
18      "address": "3 Main St.",
19   },
```

```
20 }
```

But then what are the keys to these three values? In a dictionary you can't have a value without a key.

So let's eliminate the customer id in each inner dictionary...

```
1  customers = {
2      {
3          "customer id": 0,
4          "first name":"John",
5          "last name": "Ogden",
6          "address": "301 Arbor Rd.",
7      },
8      {
9          "customer id": 1,
10         "first name":"Ann",
11         "last name": "Sattermyer",
12         "address": "PO Box 1145",
13     },
14     {
15         "customer id": 2,
16         "first name":"Jill",
17         "last name": "Somers",
18         "address": "3 Main St.",
19     },
20 }
```

...and use that value as the key for the dictionary itself...

```
1  customers = {
2      0: {
3              "first name":"John",
4              "last name": "Ogden",
5              "address": "301 Arbor Rd.",
6      },
7      1: {
8              "first name":"Ann",
9             "last name": "Sattermyer",
10             "address": "PO Box 1145",
11     },
12     2: {
13             "first name":"Jill",
14             "last name": "Somers",
15             "address": "3 Main St.",
16     },
17 }
```

Now in the **customers** dictionary, the first item has the key of 0. The value paired with this key is the first inner dictionary. The second item has the key of 1. The value is the second dictionary. Etc.

I've used sequential numbers as keys, but that's not necessary, because we're no longer using the indexing approach that we'd use for a list. As long as the keys are unique, it doesn't matter what they are. For example, they could be strings that are user names:

```
1 customers = {
2    "johnog": {
3       "first name":"John",
4       "last name": "Ogden",
5       "address": "301 Arbor Rd.",
6    },
7    "coder1200": {
8      "first name":"Ann",
9      "last name": "Sattermyer",
10     "address": "PO Box 1145",
11   },
12   "madmaxine": {
13      "first name":"Jill",
14      "last name": "Somers",
15      "address": "3 Main St.",
16   },
17 }
```

Find the interactive coding exercises for this chapter at http://www.ASmarterWayToLearn.com/python/39.html

40
How to get information out of a dictionary within another dictionary

In the last chapter I coded a dictionary, **customers**, that contained three inner dictionaries. The keys to the dictionaries were the integers **1**, **2**, and **3**. Each entire dictionary was the value that was paired with each key.

```
1 customers = {
2   0: {
3       "first name":"John",
4       "last name": "Ogden",
5       "address": "301 Arbor Rd.",
6   },
7   1: {
8       "first name":"Ann",
9       "last name": "Sattermyer",
11      "address": "PO Box 1145",
12  },
13  2: {
14      "first name":"Jill",
15      "last name": "Somers",
16      "address": "3 Main St.",
17  },
18 }
```

Previously you learned how to find the value in a dictionary by specifying its key:

```
print(customers[2])
```

The code above tells Python to display the value of the item that has a key of **2** in the **customers** dictionary. The value paired with **2** is an inner dictionary. So this is what displays:

{'first name': 'Jill', 'last name': 'Somers', 'address': '3 Main St.'}

So how do we tell Python we want, say, the address in the **2** dictionary? We say, Look in the dictionary whose key is 2…

```
print(customers[2]…
```

…and find within that dictionary the value whose key is "address"…

```
print(customers[2]["address"])
```

This displays:

3 Main St.

Find the interactive coding exercises for this chapter at
http://www.ASmarterWayToLearn.com/python/40.html

41
Functions

A *function* is a block of Python code that robotically does the same thing again and again, whenever you invoke its name. It saves you repetitive coding and makes your code easier to understand.

We'll start with a trivially simple example. Let's say you want to add two numbers and display the result:

```
1 first_number = 2
2 second_number = 3
3 total = first_number + second_number
```

The code above assigns the integer 2 to the variable **first_number** and the integer 3 to the variable **second_number**. Then it sums the values stored in the two variables and assigns the total to the third variable, **total**.

If you add this line...

```
4 print(total)
```

...Python displays the number 5.

Now I'm going to turn this code into a function:

```
1 def add_numbers():
2    first_number = 2
3    second_number = 3
4    total = first_number + second_number
5    print(total)
```

The code above defines a function named **add_numbers**. This function does exactly what the code at the beginning of this chapter does. The difference is that a function doesn't do anything until it's *called*. This is how you call the function:

```
add_numbers()
```

When Python sees the code above, it runs all the code in the function named **add_numbers**. The number 5 is displayed.

When you use functions, you always have to think of both parts, the code that defines the function and the code that calls the function. Without both parts, nothing ever happens. A definition without a call never runs. A call without a definition breaks the program.

The code that defines the function and the code that calls the function don't have to be near each other. They can be thousands of lines apart. **But note:** the function definition must come before the function call. When you call a function, Python always looks for it in the code above the call. If the function definition is below the call, Python won't find it, and you'll get an error.

Let's go over the syntax:

The definition begins with the keyword **def** (for define):

```
1 def add_numbers():
```

Then comes the name. It can be any legal variable name you like. (Technically, a function *is* a variable. This will make more sense later.)

```
1 def add_numbers():
```

The function name is followed by parentheses…

```
1 def add_numbers():
```

The line ends with a colon…

```
1 def add_numbers():
```

You indent the code that runs within the function…

```
1 def add_numbers():
2    first_number = 2
3    second_number = 3
4    total = first_number + second_number
5    print(total)
```

To run the code within the function—that is, to call the function— you write the name of the function followed by parentheses:

```
add_numbers()
```

Find the interactive coding exercises for this chapter at http://www.ASmarterWayToLearn.com/python/41.html

42
Functions: Passing them information

As you learned in the last chapter, a function is a block of code that does something robotically, whenever you invoke its name—that is, whenever you call it. For example, when you write **add_numbers()**, a function named **add_numbers** executes. To be clear: The kind of function I'm talking about is one that you've written yourself, and named yourself.

This is the code I wrote to define the **add_numbers** function:

```
1 def add_numbers():
2    first_number = 2
3    second_number = 3
4    total = first_number + second_number
5    print(total)
```

This is the code I wrote to call the function:

```
add_numbers()
```

One of the really useful things about functions is that those parentheses in the calling code…

```
add_numbers()
```

…don't have to be empty. If you put some information inside the parentheses, that information is passed to the function. The function can then use the information when it executes.

Suppose, instead of writing **add_numbers()** you write...

```
add_numbers(53, 109)
```

Now, instead of just calling the function, you're calling it and *passing data* to it. Each of the numbers inside the parentheses is known as an *argument*. In this example, you're passing two arguments to the function. Note that the two arguments are separated by a comma.

The function is now more versatile, because now it can add any two numbers you give it, not just two numbers that are hard-wired into it.

In order for a function to become a versatile robot rather than a one-job robot, you have to set it up to receive the data you're passing. Here's how you do it:

```
1 def add_numbers(first_number, second_number):
2     total = first_number + second_number
3     print(total)
```

So now we've inserted two things into the parentheses of the calling code, and also inserted two things into the parentheses of the function definition. The parentheses of the calling code contain two arguments, the numbers 53 and 109. And, as you can see in the example above, the parentheses of the function definition contain two variables, **first_number** and **second_number**. These variables store the data passed by the calling code, 53 and 109.

A variable inside the parentheses in a function definition is known as a *parameter*. The parameter name is up to you. You can give it any name that would be legal for a variable. Then you can use the variable to accomplish something in the body of the function. On line 2 in the example, I use the two parameters as the numbers to be added:

```
1 def add_numbers(first_number, second_number):
2     total = first_number + second_number
3     print(total)
```

The arguments in the function call —the numbers 53 and 109—are the information that's passed to the function by the code that calls the function. The parameters inside the parentheses in the function definition—**first_number** and **second_number**—catch the data that's passed. These variables hold the numbers 53 and 109. In other words, the numbers specified in the function call are assigned to **first_number** and **second_number** in the function. Then those parameters—i.e. those variables—are used in the body of the function.

Note that the two parameters are separated by a comma.

In the example, the numbers 53 and 109 are passed to the function by the calling code. The function adds them and displays the total, 162. Since the function accepts any two numbers as arguments, you could, for example, write…

```
add_numbers(1.11, 2.22)
```

…and Python would display the float 3.33.

But how does Python know that 1.11 goes into the parameter **first_number** and 2.22 goes into the parameter **second_number**? Simple: Since 1.11 is the first argument, it goes into the first parameter, **first_number**. Since 2.22 is the second argument, it goes into the second parameter, **second_number**.

Arguments like this are *positional* arguments—arguments that are loaded into function parameters in order, like a line of customers loaded into the cars of a theme park ride.

In the example, the arguments are two numbers, but you could put in a string, a bunch of strings, or a combination of numbers and strings. You could even put in a variable or several variables or a combination of variables, numbers, and strings. In the following code, I declare the variable **greeting** and assign it the value "Hello, there." Then, rather than using the string itself as an argument in the function call, I use the variable.

```
1 greeting = "Hello, there."
2 greet_user(greeting)
```

This is the function definition:

```
1 def greet_user(greeting):
2   print(greeting)
```

Python displays…

Hello, there.

In the example, I named the argument in the calling code **greeting**, and also named the parameter in the function code **greeting**. But this isn't necessary. The argument name and the parameter name don't have to match. No matter what an argument's name is, it is accepted by the parameter, no matter what the parameter's name is. In the following code, the variable **whatever** is the argument. The parameter **greeting** doesn't match the name, but still catches the value.

Here's the function, once again, with the parameter **greeting**.

```
1 def greet_user(greeting):
2    print(greeting)
```

And here's the statement that calls the function, with the argument **whatever**.

```
1 whatever = "Hello, there."
2 greetUser(whatever)
```

It's okay that the name of the argument and the name of the parameter don't match. The parameter still catches the argument, the string "Hello, there."

Still, it often makes sense to give an argument and a parameter the same name, for clarity.

Find the interactive coding exercises for this chapter at http://www.ASmarterWayToLearn.com/python/42.html

43
Functions: Passing information to them a different way

In the last chapter you learned that the code that calls a function can pass information—one or more arguments—to the function. Each argument is loaded into a corresponding parameter—a variable enclosed in parentheses in the first line of the function definition—in order. This matching-by-order makes the arguments *positional arguments*.

But you don't have to match arguments to parameters by order. You can code *keyword arguments*. Then the order doesn't matter. Here's a function call with two keyword arguments:

```
say_names_of_couple(husband_name="Bill", wife_name="Zelda")
```

If you write...

```
1 def say_names_of_couple(husband_name, wife_name):
2   print("The names of the couple are " + husband_name + " and " + wife_name)
```

Python displays...

The names of the couple are Bill and Zelda.

Each argument begins with a key—**husband_name** is the first one. The key is followed by an equal sign, then the value that is paired with the key, "Bill."

The function definition loads that value into the correct parameter not according to order, but by matching the key **husband_name** in the function call with **husband_name** in the function definition.

This means the order doesn't matter. You can write...

```
1 def say_names_of_couple(husband_name, wife_name):
```

...or you can reverse the order of the parameters and write...

```
1 def say_names_of_couple(wife_name, husband_name):
```

All that matters is that the name of the key in the calling code argument—**wife_name**—is the same as the parameter name in the function's definition—**wife_name**.

Find the interactive coding exercises for this chapter at http://www.ASmarterWayToLearn.com/python/43.html

44
Functions: Assigning a default value to a parameter

Let's say you code a function that calculates state sales tax on a retail sale. Using keyword arguments, you could write…

```
calc_tax(sales_total=101.37, tax_rate=.05)
```

The function would take it from there:

```
1 def calc_tax(sales_total, tax_rate):
2   print(sales_total * tax_rate)
```

When the function runs, Python displays…

5.0685

But suppose 98 percent of your sales take place in your state. Your state has a tax rate of 4%. Python allows you to make that rate the default value for the key **tax_rate**. Here's how:

```
1 def calc_tax(sales_total, tax_rate=.04):
2   print(sales_total * tax_rate)
```

Now you can skip the second argument in the function call…

```
calc_tax(sales_total=101.37, tax_rate=.05)
```

…and just write…

```
calc_tax(sales_total=101.37)
```

…and the function will have all it needs to make the calculation and display the result.

Note: Only keyword parameters can have a default value. Positional parameters can't.

In the rare case when you make a sale in another state with a different tax rate, you just put the second argument back into the function call…

```
calc_tax(sales_total=101.37, tax_rate=.075)
```

…and the function replaces the default parameter, .04, with the value passed to the function by the calling code, .075.

Note: Keyword parameters without defaults must come before keyword parameters with defaults. In the following code, **tax_rate=.04** must come after **sales_total**.

```
1 def calc_tax(sales_total, tax_rate=.04):
2   print(sales_total * tax_rate)
```

You can use an empty default parameter value for an optional argument. Let's say you have a function that prints out an order for a single product. The information includes product name, color, size, and optional engraving. Sometimes the calling code passes a string for the engraved text, and sometimes it passes nothing, when engraving hasn't been ordered. So you code the final parameter, **engraving_text**, with the default value of an empty string:

```
 def print_order(product_name, color, size,
engraving_text=""):
```

If the calling code includes engraving text as an argument, the string passed by the argument replaces the empty string. If the calling code doesn't include engraving text as an argument, the function uses the empty string—no engraving.

Find the interactive coding exercises for this chapter at http://www.ASmarterWayToLearn.com/python/44.html

45
Functions: Mixing positional and keyword arguments

You can mix positional arguments and keyword arguments. For example, you can code...

```
give_greeting("Hello there", first_name="Al")
```

The first argument is positional, because there's no keyword. The second argument is a keyword argument, because it pairs the keyword **first_name** with the value "Al."

If you code this function...

```
1 def give_greeting(greeting, first_name):
2   print(greeting + ", " + first_name)
```

...Python displays...

Hello there, Al

Be careful mixing positional and keyword arguments.

Positional arguments must come before keyword arguments.

Keyword arguments don't have to line up with parameters, but positional arguments do. If "Hello there" is the first argument and **greeting** is the second parameter, it won't work. Since the positional argument "Hello there" is the first argument, it can pass information only to the first parameter in the function defintion. **greeting** has to come first in the parameter list.

You can also throw default values into the mix. You can write...

```
give_greeting("Hello there", first_name="Al")
```

...and the code calls this function...

```
1 def give_greeting(greeting, first_name,
flattering_nickname=" the wonder boy"):
2   print(greeting + ", " + first_name +
flattering_nickname)
```

Python displays…

Hello there, Al the wonder boy

When the calling code doesn't pass an argument for
flattering_nickname, the function uses the default, "the wonder
boy".

Note: Positional arguments and parameters always come first,
keyword parameters without defaults always come second, and keyword
parameters with defaults always come last.

Lists and dictionaries, as well as strings and numbers, can be
arguments passed to a function. Here's our **customers** dictionary, a
dictionary that contains a dictionary:

```
1 customers = {
2   0: {
3         "first name":"John",
4         "last name": "Ogden",
5         "address": "301 Arbor Rd.",
6   },
7   1: {
8        "first name":"Ann",
9        "last name": "Sattermyer",
10       "address": "PO Box 1145",
11  },
12  2: {
13        "first name":"Jill",
14        "last name": "Somers",
15        "address": "3 Main St.",
16  },
17 }
```

Let's say we want to find the last name of customer 2.
This is the function call:

```
find_something(customers, 2, "last name")
```

This is the function definition:

```
1 def find_something(dict, inner_dict, target):
2    print(dict[inner_dict][target])
```

The argument **customers**—the name of the dictionary—goes into the parameter **dict**…

```
find_something(customers, 2, "last name")
```

```
1 def find_something(dict, inner_dict, target):
2    print(dict[inner_dict][target])
```

The argument **2** goes into the parameter **inner_dict**. We're looking for the inner dictionary named **2** within the outer dictionary named **customers**…

```
find_something(customers, 2, "last name")
```

```
1 def find_something(dict, inner_dict, target):
2    print(dict[inner_dict][target])
```

The argument "last name" goes into the parameter **target**. We're looking for the value whose key is "last name" in the inner dictionary…

```
find_something(customers, 2, "last name")
```

```
1 def find_something(dict, inner_dict, target):
2    print(dict[inner_dict][target])
```

The function uses the three parameters to find the value we want:

```
1 def find_something(dict, inner_dict, target):
2    print(dict[inner_dict][target])
```

Python displays…

Somers

Find the interactive coding exercises for this chapter at
http://www.ASmarterWayToLearn.com/python/45.html

46
Functions: Dealing with an unknown number of arguments

You've learned to match arguments with parameters. For every argument in the function call, you code a parameter in the function definition to store its value.

Here's a function that displays a soccer match result:

```
1 def display_result(winner, score):
2    print("The winner was " + winner)
3    print("The score was " + score)
```

If you call the function with these arguments…

```
display_result(winner="Real Madrid", score="1-0")
```

Python displays…

The winner was Real Madrid
The score was 1-0

But suppose there are times when you want to display other information about the match—but not always. For example, you call the same function and include these optional arguments:

```
display_result(winner="Real Madrid", score="1-0", overtime
="yes", injuries="none")
```

The function can handle optional arguments with this code:

```
1 def display_result(winner, score, **other_info):
```

The two asterisks followed by a parameter name mean that there may or may not be one or more extra arguments passed.

The parameter name, like any other parameter name, can be any legal variable name. You could call it…

```
1 def display_result(winner, score, **whatever):
```

How does the function handle the optional arguments? It puts them in a dictionary. The name of the dictionary is the parameter name—**other_info**, **whatever**, or whatever name follows those two asterisks.

Here's the function with code that displays any additional information:

```
1 def display_result(winner, score, **other_info):
2    print("The winner was " + winner)
3    print("The score was " + score)
4    for key, value in other_info.items():
5      print(key + ": " + value)
```

The code loops through the dictionary named **info**, displaying each item of optional information—if there is any optional information.

When Python executes the call…

```
display_result(winner="Real Madrid", score="1-0", overtime
="yes", injuries="none")
```

…this displays…

The winner was Real Madrid
The score was 1-0
overtime: yes
injuries: none

Note: Optional arguments must come after regular arguments. Optional parameters must come after regular parameters.

Positional arguments can be optional as well. To handle optional positional arguments, you use a single asterisk:

```
1 def display_nums(first_num, second_num, *opt_nums):
2    print(first_num)
3    print(second_num)
4    print(opt_nums)
```

If this is the calling code…

```
display_nums(100, 200, 300, 400, 500)
```

…100 goes into the parameter **first_num**, 200 goes into the parameter **second_num**, and the last three numbers, the optional arguments, go into the parameter ***opt_nums**. The function puts them into a tuple. I've named it **opt_nums**. Line 4 displays the tuple.

Find the interactive coding exercises for this chapter at http://www.ASmarterWayToLearn.com/python/46.html

47
Functions: Passing information back from them

You've learned how a function becomes more versatile when you pass information to it so it can deliver a custom job.

But a function can do even more. It can pass information *back* to the calling code.

Here's a function that calculates and displays sales tax:

```
1 def calc_tax(sales_total, tax_rate):
2    tax = sales_total * tax_rate
3    print(tax)
```

The calling code passes two arguments to the function:

```
calc_tax(sales_total=101.37, tax_rate=.05)
```

The function accepts these values as parameters then uses the values to do the calculation.

```
1 def calc_tax(sales_total, tax_rate):
2    tax = sales_total * tax_rate
3    print(tax)
```

When the function runs, Python displays…

5.0685

But you can remove the statement that tells Python to display the tax amount from the function…

```
1 def calc_tax(sales_total, tax_rate):
2    tax = sales_total * tax_rate
3    print(tax)
```

…and replace it with a **return** statement:

```
1 def calc_tax(sales_total, tax_rate):
2    tax = sales_total * tax_rate
3    return tax
```

You rewrite the calling statement so it has a place to put the value passed to it by the function…

```
sales_tax = calc_tax(sales_total=101.37, tax_rate=.05)
```

The statement tells Python to run the function **calc_tax** and assign the result to the variable **sales_tax**.

To display the result, you can add a **print** statement after the function call:

```
1 sales_tax = calc_tax(sales_total=101.37, tax_rate=.05)
2    print(sales_tax)
```

Python displays…

5.0685

So in order to pass information back to the calling code, you need two things. You need a final line in the function that sends the information back to the calling code…

```
3    return tax
```

…and you need a way for the calling code to accept the information. In this case, it's a variable:

```
sales_tax = calc_tax(sales_total=101.37, tax_rate=.05)
```

For brevity, you could condense these two lines of code…

```
1 sales_tax = calc_tax(sales_total=101.37, tax_rate=.05)
2 print(sales_tax)
```

…into one line of code:

```
1 print(calc_tax(sales_total=101.37, tax_rate=.05))
```

…and you could condense these three lines of code…

```
1 def calc_tax(sales_total, tax_rate):
2    tax = sales_total * tax_rate
3    return tax
```

...into two lines of code...

```
1 def calc_tax(sales_total, tax_rate):
2    return(sales_total * tax_rate)
```

Find the interactive coding exercises for this chapter at
http://www.ASmarterWayToLearn.com/python/47.html

48
Using functions as variables (which is what they really are)

In the last chapter, I may have confused you when I said you could condense...

```
1 sales_tax = calc_tax(sales_total=101.37, tax_rate=.05)
2   print(sales_tax)
```

...into...

```
print(calc_tax(sales_total=101.37, tax_rate=.05))
```

In the longer, two-line code, the variable **sales_tax** receives the value returned by the function **calc_tax**. Then the variable is used in the **print** statement to tell Python the value to display.

In the condensed statement, it appears that I'm telling Python to display the function! But really, I'm telling Python to display the value that's returned by the function. Instead of enclosing a variable in the parentheses, I'm enclosing the function. This is legal, because a function *is* a variable.

Here's another example. Let's say I write a function that adds two numbers...

```
1 def add_numbers(first_number, second_number):
2   return first_number + second_number
```

...and another function that subtracts two numbers...

```
1 def subtract_numbers(first_number, second_number):
2   return first_number - second_number
```

Suppose I write...

```
1 result_of_adding = add_numbers(1, 2)
2 result_of_subtracting = subtract_numbers(3, 2)
3 sum_of_results = result_of_adding + result_of_subtracting
```

Line 1 calls the first function. The result, 3, is returned and placed in **result_of_adding**.

Line 2 calls the second function. The result, 1, is returned and placed in **result_of_subtracting**.

Line 3 totals the values stored in the two variables, 4, and assigns the sum to **sum_of_results**.

This can all be condensed into one line by replacing the two variables with the functions themselves:

```
1 sum_of_results = add_numbers(1, 2) + subtract_numbers(3, 2)
```

Find the interactive coding exercises for this chapter at http://www.ASmarterWayToLearn.com/python/48.html

49
Functions: Local vs. global variables

Now we come to the subject of variable *scope*. That is, the difference between *global* and *local* variables. Some variables have global scope, which makes them global variables. Other variables have local scope, which makes them local variables.

A global variable is one you define in the main body of your code—that is, *not* in a function.

```
what_to_say = "Hi"
```

A local variable is one that you define in a function.

```
1 def say_something():
2    what_to_say = "Hi"
```

What makes a global variable global is that it is recognized everywhere in your code. Global scope is like global fame. Wherever you go in the world, they've heard of the pope.

A local variable is one that's recognized only within the function that introduces it. Local scope is like local fame. The mayor of Duluth is known only in Duluth.

Let's say you write, in your main code...

```
what_to_say = "Hi"
```

... you can use the variable anywhere.
But if you write, in a function...

```
1 def say_something():
2    what_to_say = "Hi"
```

...and you try to use the variable **what_to_say** in your main code or in another function...

```
print(what_to_say)
```

...Python doesn't recognize the variable. You get an error message:

NameError: name 'what_to_say' is not defined....

In the following code, **b**, **c**, and **total** are local.

```
1 def whatever(b, c):
2   total = b + c
3   return total
```

If, outside the function, you write…

```
print(a)
```

or…

```
print(c)
```

…or…

```
print(total)
```

…you'll get an error message.

On the other hand, if you write the **print** statements within the function where they're defined…

```
1 def whatever(b, c):
2   total = b + c
3   print(a)
4   print(b)
5   print(total)
```

…Python has no problem. A variable defined in a function is recognized inside the function—and only inside the function.

Code outside a function can't use variables defined inside the function, but code inside the function can use variables defined in the main code. Remember, variables defined in the main code are global, meaning that they're recognized everywhere, including inside functions. So if you write…

```
a = 2
```

…then you write…

```
def display_number()
  print(a)
```

…it'll work.

However, good coders avoid using global variables inside functions, because it's confusing. It's better to pass values to functions using arguments. It's better to keep all the variables used in functions local.

Now look at this code, a function definition and three statements outside the function:

```
1 def whatever():
2     y = 2
3     print(y)

100 y = 1
101 whatever()
102 print(y)
```

The function defines **y** as 2. Later, the main code defines **y** as 1. Next, it calls the function. After the function call, line 102 displays the value of **y**.

On line 3 the function displays the value of **y** as it's defined inside the function—the value 2. After the function runs, you might think that line 102 of the main code would display **y** as 2 also, because, after all, the function assigned **y** the value 2, and it did this after the main code assigned **y** the value 1. But that's not what happens.

The function displays the value 2, and then the main code displays the value 1. This is because **y** is two different variables that (confusingly) happen to have the same name! Inside the function, **y** is a local variable because the function assigns it a value. This variable called **y** is unknown outside the function. What happens to the local variable **y** inside the function doesn't affect the global variable **y** outside the function. The global variable retains the value of 1 that it was assigned on line 100.

Find the interactive coding exercises for this chapter at:
http://www.ASmarterWayToLearn.com/python/49.html

50
Functions within functions

Within a function, you can call other functions.

Let's look at a trivial example, to keep things simple.

Recall the example in the last chapter:

```
100 def say_something():
200    what_to_say = "Hi"
300    print(what_to_say)
```

You could break this up into two functions. The function, **say_something**, calls another function, **now_say_it** ...

```
100 def say_something():
200    what_to_say = "Hi"
300    now_say_it()
```

This is the function that's called by **say_something**:

```
1 def now_say_it():
2    print(what_to_say)
```

Note: The function that is called must be earlier in your code than the function that calls it.

But there's a problem with this code.

You learned in the last chapter that a variable assigned a value inside a function—a local variable—is only recognized inside the function itself. Outside the function, it isn't known.

Since the **variable what_to_say** is defined inside **say_something**, the variable belongs to **say_something** and is known only that function. So it isn't recognized inside the **now_say_it** function.

When you write...

```
1 def now_say_it():
2    print(what_to_say)
```

...you get an error message.

You need to pass the value of **say_something**'s variable

what_to_say to **now_say_it** as an argument:

```
100 def say_something():
200    what_to_say = "Hi"
300    now_say_it(what_to_say)
```

...and **now_say_it** must receive it as a parameter...

```
1 def now_say_it(content):
2    print(content)
```

I could have given the parameter in **now_say_it** the same name as the argument, **what_to_say**, passed to it by **say_something**. But I gave the parameter a different name, **content**, to emphasize that the argument passed by **say_something** and the parameter that receives it in **now_say_it** aren't the same variable, even though you might give them the same names. That's because they're both local variables, known only inside their functions, no matter what names you give them.

Find the interactive coding exercises for this chapter at:
http://www.ASmarterWayToLearn.com/python/50.html

51
While loops

A **for** loop, as you learned, cycles through a series of things, repeating itself until it comes to the end of the series, or until it encounters a **break** statement.

For example, you have a list of clean cities:

```
cleanest_cities = ["Cheyenne", "Santa Fe", "Tucson", "Great
Falls", "Honolulu"]
```

The user enters the name of a city...

```
city_to_check = input("Enter the name of a city: ")
```

The loop then cycles through the list of clean cities, checking to see if there's a match:

```
1 for a_clean_city in cleanest_cities:
2   if city_to_check == a_clean_city:
3     print("It's one of the cleanest cities")
4     break
```

But suppose you want the user to be able to check a city, and then if she wants, check another city after that, and then another city after that, etc.

For this, you use a **while** loop:

```
1 user_input = ""
2 while user_input != "q":
3   user_input = input("Enter a city, or q to quit:")
4   if user_input != "q":
5     for a_clean_city in cleanest_cities:
6       if user_input == a_clean_city:
7         print("It's one of the cleanest cities")
8         break
```

On line 1 the variable **user_input** is assigned an initial value of ""—an empty string:

```
1 user_input = ""
2 while user_input != "q":
3   user_input = input("Enter a city, or q to quit:")
4   if user_input != "q":
5     for a_clean_city in cleanest_cities:
6       if user_input == a_clean_city:
7         print("It's one of the cleanest cities")
8         break
```

Line 2 says, "For as long as the user hasn't entered "q," keep executing the code that follows:"

```
1 user_input = ""
2 while user_input != "q":
3   user_input = input("Enter a city, or q to quit:")
4   if user_input != "q":
5     for a_clean_city in cleanest_cities:
6       if user_input == a_clean_city:
7         print("It's one of the cleanest cities")
8         break
```

In Line 3 Python prompts for the user's input, and places it in the variable **user_input**.

```
1 user_input = ""
2 while user_input != "q":
3   user_input = input("Enter a city, or q to quit:")
4   if user_input != "q":
5     for a_clean_city in cleanest_cities:
6       if user_input == a_clean_city:
7         print("It's one of the cleanest cities")
8         break
```

If the user has entered anything other than "q"…

```
1 user_input = ""
2 while user_input != "q":
3   user_input = input("Enter a city, or q to quit:")
4   if user_input != "q":
5     for a_clean_city in cleanest_cities:
6       if user_input == a_clean_city:
7         print("It's one of the cleanest cities")
8         break
```

…Python loops through the list of cleanest cities, trying to find a match with the city that the user entered:

```
1 user_input = ""
2 while user_input != "q":
3   user_input = input("Enter a city, or q to quit:")
4   if user_input != "q":
5     for a_clean_city in cleanest_cities:
6       if user_input == a_clean_city:
7         print("It's one of the cleanest cities")
8         break
```

The **for** loop either finds a match or it doesn't. In either case, Python goes back to line 2, checking to see if "q" has been entered. If "q" hasn't been entered, the prompt executes again. If "q" has been entered, the **while** loop ends.

Things to remember:

- You have to assign a value to the variable that the **while** loop depends on, in this case **user_input**, before you start the **while** loop. Otherwise, the first time through, before the user has entered anything, Python doesn't recognize the variable when you ask it to check its value in line 2. In this example, the value is an empty string.

- As always, when a block of code is controlled by code above it, the dependent block is indented. All the statements below line 2 are controlled by line 2's **while** statement, so they're indented. All the statements below line 4 are controlled by line 4's **if** statement, so they're indented. All the statements below line 5 are controlled by line 5's **for** statement, so they're indented. All the statements below line 6 are controlled by line 6's **if** statement, so they're indented.

Find the interactive coding exercises for this chapter at: http://www.ASmarterWayToLearn.com/python/51.html

52
While loops: Setting a flag

In the last chapter you learned to use a **while** loop to keep repeating something until the user enters "q" for "quit."

```
1 user_input = ""
2 while user_input != "q":
3   user_input = input("Enter a city, or q to quit:")
4   if user_input != "q":
5     for a_clean_city in cleanest_cities:
6       if user_input == a_clean_city:
7         print("It's one of the cleanest cities")
8         break
```

I'm going to modify this code to show you how to use a *flag*. I'll highlight the changed code:

```
1 keep_looping = True
2 while keep_looping == True:
3   user_input = input("Enter a city, or q to quit:")
4   if user_input != "q":
5     for a_clean_city in cleanest_cities:
6       if user_input == a_clean_city:
7         print("It's one of the cleanest cities")
8         break
9   else:
10    keep_looping = False
```

Line 1 assigns **True** to the variable that I named **keep_looping**. **True** is a special value known as a *Boolean*. I'll get back to that.

Line 2 says, "As long as the variable **keep_looping** stays **True**, keep looping."

The code inside the loop is the same as it was in the last chapter.

Lines 9 and 10 say, "If the user has entered 'q,' change the value of **keep_looping** to **False**."

Since the loop continues only as long as **keep_looping** has a value of **True**, the loop ends.

There are only two Booleans, **True** and **False**.

Things to remember:

- **True** and **False** aren't enclosed in quotation marks. They aren't strings.

- They must be capitalized.

Find the interactive coding exercises for this chapter at: http://www.ASmarterWayToLearn.com/python/52.html

53
Classes

On your first visit to a health clinic, the receptionist hands you a clipboard with a form clipped to it. You fill out the form to provide your personal information.

Why a form? Why doesn't she just give you a blank sheet of paper with the instructions, "Tell us about yourself"?

You know the answer. The clinic wants a standard set of information organized the same way for each patient. The form is a template that makes things easier for both you and the clinic. It standardizes and organizes information so the information is easier to access and easier to work with.

In Python, *classes* are templates. They help you standardize and organize information.

When you write the first line of code creating a class …

```
1 class Patient():
2     etc...
```

…you're saying to Python, "I'm creating a class that I'm naming **Patient**. Use this class as the template for each virtual sheet of information about a bunch of different patients. Each patient will have her own *instance* of this form, but the information for all patients is to be structured the same way."

A class is like the health clinic receptionist's tablet of forms. Before it's filled out, each sheet in the tablet is identical to all the others. When a patient fills out a copy, it still has the same structure as all the others but contains unique particulars.

Coding the first line of a class definition is like creating a title at the top of a form:

Patient

Things to notice about this first line of code that defines a class:
It begins with the keyword **class**.

```
1 class Patient():
2   etc...
```

Then comes the name you're giving it. Naming rules here follow those for variables. The only difference is that by custom, a class name begins with a capital letter:

```
1 class Patient():
2   etc...
```

The class name is followed by a pair of parentheses and a colon:

```
1 class Patient():
2   etc...
```

Find the interactive coding exercises for this chapter at:
http://www.ASmarterWayToLearn.com/python/53.html

54
Classes: Starting to build the structure

The first line of code...

```
1 class Patient():
```

...tells Python that we're creating a class, a kind of template. The template will structure each instance, that is, each individual patient record.

To begin with, we know that each patient's record contains a last name. So let's start there:

```
1 class Patient():
2    def __init__(self, last_name):
```

Line 2 creates an *attribute*—a chunk of information to be provided about each patient:

Patient

Last Name _____

When you become a full-fledged computer scientist, you can come back and explain to me the deeper meaning of
def __init__(self,.... In the meantime, let's just say that it's always the same abracadabra:

It's the keyword **def**…

```
1 class Patient():
2   def __init__(self, last_name):
```

…followed by 2 underscores, the keyword **init**, then 2 more underscores…

```
1 class Patient():
2   def __init__(self, last_name):
```

…an opening parenthesis, the keyword **self**, and a comma…

```
1 class Patient():
2   def __init__(self, last_name):
```

Then comes the name of an attribute to include in each individual patient record. In this case, it's the last name of the patient:

```
1 class Patient():
2   def __init__(self, last_name):
```

Line 2 ends with a closing parenthesis and colon:

```
1 class Patient():
2   def __init__(self, last_name):
```

Note that line 2 is indented.

Find the interactive coding exercises for this chapter at:
http://www.ASmarterWayToLearn.com/python/54.html

55
Classes: A bit of housekeeping

We've told Python we're defining a class named **Patient**...

```
1 class Patient():
```

...and we've started to structure the class, specifying that it is to contain an attribute named **last_name**...

```
1 class Patient():
2   def __init__(self, last_name):
```

Next, we have to write a line that Python needs in order to keep things straight. It's just housekeeping. We need to tell Python that in each instance that we create using the class as a template, there will be a variable that has the same value as the attribute we're talking about in line 2, **last_name**.

You can give this attribute any name you like, as long as it's legal...

```
1 class Patient():
2   def __init__(self, last_name):
3     self.whatever_dude = last_name
```

But the easy thing to do is to duplicate the attribute name. That's what I'll ask you to do in the exercises.

```
1 class Patient():
2   def __init__(self, last_name):
3     self.last_name = last_name
```

You may wonder why it's necessary to tell Python that the **last_name** in line 3 has the same value as the **last_name** in line 2. That's another one you can explain to me when you're teaching at Stanford.

Note that line 3 has to start with that mysterious **self**, followed by a dot...

```
1 class Patient():
2    def __init__(self, last_name):
3        self.last_name = last_name
```

Note also that line 3 is indented one level deeper than line 2.

Find the interactive coding exercises for this chapter at:
http://www.ASmarterWayToLearn.com/python/55.html

56
Classes: Creating an instance

We've created a class called **Patient**...

```
1 class Patient():
2   def __init__(self, last_name):
3     self.last_name = last_name
```

A class is analogous to the blank form a healthcare receptionist hands you to fill out. The form is the same for everyone. What differs from copy to copy is what you write in the blanks.

For learning purposes, our paper form has only on blank to fill, **Last Name**.

Patient

Last Name _____

Similarly, our class, **Patient**, has only one attribute to fill in, **last_name**.

One more thing, though. In addition to the single blank for the last name, the paper form includes a unique identifier for each patient. The printer might have added this automatically, with a different number for

each individual sheet. This sheet's unique identifier, the patient ID, is
pid4044.

Patient
pid4343

Last Name _____

So now we fill in the single blank for patient pid343:

Patient
pid4343

Last Name Taleb _____

Here's how we do the same thing by creating an instance of the class
Patient:

```
pid4343 = Patient("Taleb")
```

pid4343 is the unique identifier for this particular patient. It's just a variable, which means I made it up. But it does need to be different for each instance that we create for the class, because it's a *unique* identifier. No two patients can share the same identifier.

When we write…

```
pid4343 = Patient("Taleb")
```

…we're saying, "Create a copy (instance) of the **Patient** form (class) that has the unique identifier **pid4343**, and fill in the blank for last name (**last_name** attribute) with "Taleb."

In this one-attribute class that we're starting with, we don't have to tell Python which "blank" to fill in, because at this point, our class has only one attribute, **last_name**.

When we create an instance of a class—a fresh sheet to fill out—we say we *instantiate* the class.

We begin with the name of the instance—its unique identifier. In this instance, it's **pid4343**.

```
pid4343 = Patient("Taleb")
```

Then comes the equal sign:

```
pid4343 = Patient("Taleb")
```

Then the name of the class:

```
pid4343 = Patient("Taleb")
```

Then the value to be assigned to the attribute, in parentheses:

```
pid4343 = Patient("Taleb")
```

We can use the class to create as many instances—as many filled-out forms—as we need:

```
pid4344 = Patient("Anand")

pid4345 = Patient("Oppenheimer")

pid4346 = Patient("Lin")

pid12902 = Patient("Nilsson")
```

Now we have the equivalent of five filled-out forms for five different patients. The particulars are different, but the structure is identical.

Instead of creating a class and then creating multiple instances of the class, you could create a dictionary for each patient:

```
pid4343 = {"last name": "Taleb"}

pid4344 = {"last name": "Anand"}

pid4345 = {"last name": "Oppenheimer"}

pid4346 = {"last name": "Lin"}

pid12902 = {"last name": "Nilsson"}
```

This works, but it's the equivalent of the clinic receptionist creating a new patient form from scratch for each patient. That might make sense for our ridiculously simple form with only one piece of patient information in it, but the slight extra effort required to create a class pays off in ways you'll appreciate when you're working with more complex sets of data.

Find the interactive coding exercises for this chapter at: http://www.ASmarterWayToLearn.com/python/56.html

57
Classes: A little more complexity

We created a class named **Patient**, with just a single attribute,
last_name:

```
1 class Patient():
2   def __init__(self, last_name):
3     self.last_name = last_name
```

Then we instantiated the class five times. These were the instances
we created:

```
pid4343 = Patient("Taleb")

pid4344 = Patient("Anand")

pid4345 = Patient("Oppenheimer")

pid4346 = Patient("Lin")

pid12902 = Patient("Nilsson")
```

Let's add two more attributes to the class to make it slightly more
realistic:

```
1 class Patient():
2   def __init__(self, last_name, first_name, age):
3     self.last_name = last_name
4     self.first_name = first_name
5     self.age = age
```

Here are five instances of this more complicated class:

```
pid4343 = Patient("Taleb", "Sue", 61)

pid4344 = Patient("Anand", "Punya", 29)

pid4345 = Patient("Oppenheimer", "Douglas", 15)

pid4346 = Patient("Lin", "Lilly", 48)

pid12902 = Patient("Nilsson", "Rhonda", 33)
```

Note that in each instance, there's a value that matches up with each attribute in the class definition on line 2. "Taleb" matches up with **last_name**, "Sue" matches up with **first_name**, 61 matches up with **age**.

Python matches the values with the attributes according to their order. It works like positional arguments—the arguments in a function call that match up with the parameters in the function, according to their order.

last_name is the first attribute...

```
1 class Patient():
2    def __init__(self, last_name, first_name, age):
```

...and Python knows to match "Taleb" with it because "Taleb" is the first value...

```
pid4343 = Patient("Taleb", "Sue", 61)
```

first_name is the second attribute...

```
1 class Patient():
2    def __init__(self, last_name, first_name, age):
```

...and "Sue" is the second value...

```
pid4343 = Patient("Taleb", "Sue", 61)
```

age is the third attribute...

```
1 class Patient():
2    def __init__(self, last_name, first_name, age):
```

...and 61 is the third value...

```
pid4343 = Patient("Taleb", "Sue", 61)
```

It's that simple.

Find the interactive coding exercises for this chapter at: http://www.ASmarterWayToLearn.com/python/57.html

58
Classes: Getting info out of instances

We created an instance of the class **Patient** for **pid4343** that had three attributes: **last_name**, **first_name**, and **age**. The values matching these attribute names were "Taleb", "Sue", and 61.

Here's how we get Sue Taleb's age out of her patient record:

```
age_of_patient = pid4343.age
```

The line above assigns Sue Taleb's age, 61, to a variable I've named **age_of_patient**.

Note the syntax. It starts with the unique identifier of the instance...

```
age_of_patient = pid4343.age
```

Then there's a dot...

```
age_of_patient = pid4343.age
```

And the name of the attribute...

```
age_of_patient = pid4343.age
```

If I just wanted to display Sue Taleb's age, I could write...

```
print(pid4343.age)
```

Python displays...

61

Find the interactive coding exercises for this chapter at:
http://www.ASmarterWayToLearn.com/python/58.html

59
Classes: Building functions into them

Our **Patient** class has three attributes: **last_name**, **first_name**, and **age**. Each instance of the class contains values that match these attributes…

```
pid4343 = Patient("Taleb", "Sue", 61)
```

Here's a function that checks the age of a patient and displays a message if the patient is under 21:

```
1 def say_if_minor(patient_first_name, patient_last_name,
patient_age):
2  if patient_age < 21:
3    print(patient_first_name + " " + patient_last_name + "
is a minor")
```

This is the code that calls the function, passing the three attributes of patient **pid4343** as arguments:

```
say_if_minor(pid4343.first_name, pid4343.last_name,
pid4343.age)
```

Rather than coding a freestanding function, we can build the function into the class itself. When we do that, the function is called a *method*. In the next chapter I'll show you how to code it. But look how simple it is to call the function when it's built-in:

```
pid4343.say_if_minor()
```

It starts with the name of the instance…

```
pid4343…
```

…which is connected by a dot to the name of the method…

```
pid4343.say_if_minor()
```

Without your specifying the attributes of **pid4343**, the method receives all of them.

This code that calls a freestanding function…

```
say_if_minor(pid4343.first_name, pid4343.last_name,
pid4343.age)
```

…and this code that calls a method…

```
pid4343.say_if_minor()
```

…produce exactly the same result.

As I said, when you call a method, it receives all the attributes of an instance without your having to explicitly pass those values to the method as arguments. But in addition, you can pass arguments to a method the same way you'd pass arguments to a freestanding function:

```
pid4343.say_if_minor("April", insured=True)
```

In the code above, there are two arguments: **"April"**, a positional argument, and **insured=True**, a keyword argument.

Find the interactive coding exercises for this chapter at: http://www.ASmarterWayToLearn.com/python/59.html

60
Classes: Coding a method

This is the freestanding function that you saw in the last chapter:

```
1 def say_if_minor(patient_first_name, patient_last_name,
patient_age):
2   if patient_age < 21:
3     print(patient_first_name + " " + patient_last_name + "
is a minor")
```

The code that calls the function passes three arguments to it...

```
say_if_minor(pid4343.first_name, pid4343.last_name,
pid4343.age)
```

...and these arguments arc loaded into the function's three parameters...

```
1 def say_if_minor(patient_first_name, patient_last_name,
patient_age):
2   if patient_age < 21:
3     print(patient_first_name + " " + patient_last_name + "
is a minor")
```

But when you call a method within a class, you don't pass attributes to the method. Since the method is part of the instance definition that also includes the attribute values, the method already knows those values.

```
pid4343.say_if_minor()
```

...yet the method receives all the attributes of the instance, in this case **pid4343**.

Here's the **Patient** class with the method added:

```
1 class Patient():
2  def __init__(self, last_name, first_name, age):
3    self.last_name = last_name
4    self.first_name = first_name
5    self.age = age
6  def say_if_minor(self):
7    if self.age < 21:
8      print("This patient is a minor")
```

It's similar to the freestanding function, but instead of writing…

```
1 def say_if_minor(pid4343.first_name, pid4343.last_name,
pid4343.age)
```

…you write…

```
6    def say_if_minor(self):
```

self refers to the instance and all its attributes. In our example, it refers to the instance **pid4343** that the method call starts with…

```
pid4343.say_if_minor()
```

Since **self** refers to the instance **pid4343**, if you write **self.first_name**, the method knows you're referring to the **first_name** attribute of **pid4343**, "Sue". If you write **self.last_name**, the method knows you're referring to the **last_name** attribute of **pid4343**, "Taleb". If you write **self.age**, the method knows you're referring to the **age** attribute of **pid4343**, 61.

See how lines 7 and 8 use those values:

```
1 class Patient():
2  def __init__(self, last_name, first_name, age):
3    self.last_name = last_name
4    self.first_name = first_name
5    self.age = age
6  def say_if_minor(self):
7    if self.age < 21:
8      print(self.first_name + " " + self.last_name + " is
a minor")
```

About indentation: Note that the first line of the method definition is indented two levels, like the attribute definitions on lines 3 through 6. The body of the method definition is indented further.

To review:

The first line of a method definition always takes the same single parameter, **self**:

```
6   def say_if_minor(self):
```

All of the attributes of the instance are available to the method when you connect **self** by a dot with the attribute names:

```
7      if self.age < 21:
8         print(self.first_name + " " + self.last_name + " is
a minor")
```

Find the interactive coding exercises for this chapter at:
http://www.ASmarterWayToLearn.com/python/60.html

61
Classes: Changing an attribute's value

pid4343, Sue Taleb, has remarried. Her new last name is Ortega. We need to revise her record.

You already know how to target an attribute of a class instance:

```
pid4343.last_name
```

Changing the value of the patient's **last_name** attribute is as easy as this:

```
pid4343.last_name = "Ortega"
```

Here's a method that does the same thing:

```
1 class Patient():
2   def __init__(self, last_name, first_name, age):
3     self.last_name = last_name
4     self.first_name = first_name
5     self.age = age
6   def say_if_minor(self):
7     if self.age < 21:
8       print("This patient is a minor")
9   def change_last_name(self, new_last_name):
10    self.last_name = new_last_name
```

Lines 9 and 10 define a method named **change_last_name**.

Unlike the **say_if_minor** method defined in lines 6-8, this method includes a parameter in addition to the required **self**. I've named this parameter **new_last_name**...

```
1 class Patient():
2  def __init__(self, last_name, first_name, age):
3     self.last_name = last_name
4     self.first_name = first_name
5     self.age = age
6  def say_if_minor(self):
7     if self.age < 21:
8       print("This patient is a minor")
9  def change_last_name(self, new_last_name):
10    self.last_name = new_last_name
```

The calling code passes the value "Ortega" to the method. The value goes into the parameter **new_last_name**. And the value is assigned to the **last_name** attribute of the instance…

```
1 class Patient():
2  def __init__(self, last_name, first_name, age):
3     self.last_name = last_name
4     self.first_name = first_name
5     self.age = age
6  def say_if_minor(self):
7     if self.age < 21:
8       print("This patient is a minor")
9  def change_last_name(self, new_last_name):
10    self.last_name = new_last_name
```

This is the calling code:

```
pid4343.change_last_name("Ortega")
```

It starts with the name of the instance…

```
pid4343.change_last_name("Ortega")
```

There's a dot followed by the name of the method…

```
pid4343.change_last_name("Ortega")
```

…and, inside the parentheses, the argument to be passed to the method…

```
pid4343.change_last_name("Ortega")
```

Find the interactive coding exercises for this chapter at:
http://www.ASmarterWayToLearn.com/python/61.html

62
Data files

In all the coding so far in this book, none of the data has been preserved. We created variables, lists, dictionaries, and class instances that contained information, but as soon as the computer was turned off, all of it disappeared.

You know how to save a word processing document or spreadsheet, but how do you save data processed by Python?

It starts with a line of Python code:

```
with open("whatever.txt", "w") as file_to_work_with:
```

This line opens the text file *whatever.txt* if such a file exists. If it doesn't exist, Python creates it.

Here's the breakdown.

with is a puzzling (to me) way to tell Python to close the file after you write to it...

```
with open("whatever.txt", "w") as file_to_work_with:
```

open is easy to remember...

```
with open("whatever.txt", "w") as file_to_work_with:
```

The first item inside the parentheses is the name of the text file, in quotes...

```
with open("whatever.txt", "w") as file_to_work_with:
```

Then a comma, followed by **"w"**. It tells Python that you're opening the file so you can write to it...

```
with open("whatever.txt", "w") as file_to_work_with:
```

as is a keyword meaning that you're assigning a *file handle* to the file. In addition to the file name, "whatever.text," Python needs a handle in order to get into the file. In this case, I've given it a handle of **file_to_work_with**.

```
with open("whatever.txt", "w") as file_to_work_with:
```

The line ends with a colon, promising that there's more code to come…

```
with open("whatever.txt", "w") as file_to_work_with:
```

You could open the file without the initial **with**, opting to close the file yourself when you're ready…

```
file_to_work_with = open("whatever.txt", "w"):
```

…but I like the automatic-closing feature, because it's one less thing to remember, and removes the possibility that you'll fail to close the door behind you.

Note that the designation **"whatever.txt"** assumes that the file is in the same folder as the Python program that's opening it. If it isn't in the same folder, you must include the path. For example, if *whatever.txt* is in the *data* subfolder of the Python folder and you're using Windows, you would write…

```
with open("data\whatever.txt", "w") as file_to_work_with:
```

On OS X and Linux, you'd use a forward slash:

```
with open("data/whatever.txt", "w") as file_to_work_with:
```

Note that the handle **file_to_work_with** is a name that I made up. You can use any name you like, as long as it's a legal variable name…

```
with open("whatever.txt", "w") as f:
```

Find the interactive coding exercises for this chapter at: http://www.ASmarterWayToLearn.com/python/62.html

63
Data files: Storing data

Let's store the string "Hello world!" in a file.

First we open a file:

```
with open("greet.txt", "w") as f:
```

"greet.txt" is the file name. **f** is the handle we're choosing to give it.

If the file *greet.txt* exists, the code above opens it. If the file *greet.text* doesn't exist, the code above creates it.

Now we write a second line that stores the string in the file:

```
1 with open("greet.txt", "w") as f:
2   f.write("Hello, world!")
```

In these two lines of code, we've opened (or created) a file named *greet.txt*, stored the string "Hello, world!" in it, and (automatically, thanks to **with** on line 1) closed it.

Note that if the *greet.txt* is an existing file, any text in the file is overwritten with "Hello world!" Later, you'll learn how to append data to an existing file, but when you specify "w" in line 1…

```
1 with open("greet.txt", "w") as f:
2   f.write("Hello, world!")
```

…you're telling Python to replace any data that's already in the file. Line 2 begins with the file handle you specified in line 1…

```
1 with open("greet.txt", "w") as f:
2   f.write("Hello, world!")
```

Then a dot followed by the keywork **write**…

```
1 with open("greet.txt", "w") as f:
2   f.write("Hello, world!")
```

The string that we're storing in the file is in parentheses…

```
1 with open("greet.txt", "w") as f:
2    f.write("Hello, world!")
```

It also works if the string is stored in a variable:

```
1 greeting = "Hello, world!"
2 with open("greet.txt", "w") as f:
3    f.write(greeting)
```

Find the interactive coding exercises for this chapter at:
http://www.ASmarterWayToLearn.com/python/63.html

64
Data files: Retrieving data

There's a text file, *greet.txt*. Its entire contents: the string "Hello world!"

How do we retrieve those contents? First we open the file:

```
1 with open("greet.txt", "r") as f:
```

Note that the only difference between opening a file to write to it and opening a file to read from it is this...

```
1 with open("greet.txt", "r") as f:
```

We specify "**r**" for "read" instead of "**w**" for "write."

Then we read the file, loading its contents into a variable...

```
1 with open("greet.txt", "r") as f:
2    text_of_file = f.read()
```

The string "Hello, World!" is now stored in the variable **text_of_file**.

Note that **text_of_file** is a name I made up. You could use any legal variable name.

If you write...

```
print(text_of_file)
```

...Python displays...

Hello, World!

The read-file mode is the default for the **open** statement, so if you're opening a file to read data, you can, if you like, skip the "r" and just write...

```
1 with open("greet.txt", "r") as f:
```

Find the interactive coding exercises for this chapter at:
http://www.ASmarterWayToLearn.com/python/64.html

65
Data files: Appending data

When you specify **"w"**…

```
with open("greet.txt", "w") as f:
```

…the data that you write to the file overwrites any data that the file already contains.

To append data to a file while preserving existing data in the file, you write…

```
with open("greet.txt", "a") as f:
```

So let's say the data in the greet.txt file is, in its entirety, "Hello, World!"

If you write…

```
1 with open("greet.txt", "a") as f:
2   f.write("\nHave a nice day!")
```

…the contents of the file are now "Hello, World!\nHave a nice day!"

\n is the new-line character. The text that follows **\n** is placed on a new line. So if you write..

```
1 with open("greet.txt") as f:
2   message = f.read()
3   print(message)
```

…Python displays…

Hello, World!
Have a nice day!

Find the interactive coding exercises for this chapter at:
http://www.ASmarterWayToLearn.com/python/65.html

66
Modules

In the chapters dealing with functions, you learned how to define a function and how to call it. The function definitions were in the same Python file as the function calls. That is, they were in your main Python program.

An alternative is to store some or all functions in separate Python files. These files are called *modules*.

Like any Python file, a module has a filename extension of *.py*. For example, *calculations.py*.

You can store functions, classes, and more in a module. Most commonly, modules are used to store functions.

What's good about modules:

- Write a function once, call it from any Python program.

- Keep your main programs shorter and simpler to read.

- Use code written by other people by importing their modules.

It takes just one line in your main program to make all the code in *calculations.py* available to your main program:

```
import calculations
```

Note that you omit the filename extension *.py*.

Let's say you have a function in your main program that calculates tax from your main code…

```
1 def calc_tax(sales_total, tax_rate):
2    tax = sales_total * tax_rate
3    return tax
```

You remove the function from your main program and place it in a module named *calculations.py*.

The function code remains the same. But instead of the calling code you would use if the function were in the main program…

```
tax_for_this_order = calc_tax(sales_total=101.37,
tax_rate=.05)
```

You let Python know that the function is in the module named *calculations.py*...

```
tax_for_this_order =
calculations.calc_tax(sales_total=101.37, tax_rate=.05)
```

You've already imported the module, so Python knows exactly what to do.

Find the interactive coding exercises for this chapter at:
http://www.ASmarterWayToLearn.com/python/66.html

67
CSV files

CSV files are text-only files that are simplified versions of a spreadsheet or database. "CSV" stands for "Comma-Separated Values."

If you have an Excel file...

	A	B	C
1	**Year**	**Event**	**Winner**
2	1995	Best-Kept Lawn	None
3	1999	Gobstones	Welch National
4	2006	World Cup	Burkina Faso

...you can export it from Excel as a CSV file.
The CSV file looks like this...

```
Year,Event,Winner
1995,Best-Kept Lawn,None
1999,Gobstones,Welch National
2006,World Cup,Burkina Faso
```

Each row of the spreadsheet is a separte line in the CSV file.
Within each row, each cell is separated by a comma.

Notice that the formatting in the Excel file has disappeared in the CSV file. A CSV file is nothing but text.

To work with a CSV file in a Python program, you begin by importing Python's built-in *csv* module:

```
import csv
```

This module is included in Python 3. If Python 3 is on your system, you've got the module, ready to go.

So let's say you've exported the Excel spreadsheet above as *competitions.csv.*

To read the file in Python, you begin with the usual line 1:

```
1 with open("competitions.csv") as f:
```

This is the same syntax you learned for opening a text file.

Remember, **f** is a name I've chosen for the file handle. You could use any legal variable name.

The following code…

```
1 with open("competitions.csv") as f:
2     contents_of_file = csv.reader(f)
```

…calls a function, **reader**, in the *csv* module and passes the argument **f** to the function. **f** is the file handle we've chosen for the file we've opened, *competitions.csv*. That's the file we're asking the function to read.

The function returns the contents of the file. I've named the variable that receives the contents **contents_of_file**.

```
1 with open("competitions.csv") as f:
2     contents_of_file = csv.reader(f)
```

Find the interactive coding exercises for this chapter at:
http://www.ASmarterWayToLearn.com/python/67.html

68
CSV files: Reading them

You've opened the file *competitions.csv* and assigned it a file handle, **f**. Python will use this handle to access the contents of the file:

```
1 with open("competitions.csv") as f:
```

You've called the function **csv.reader**, with the argument, **(f)**, and assigned the file content that comes back from the function to a variable, **contents_of_f**.

```
2    contents_of_f = csv.reader(f)
```

The contents of the CSV file returned by the **csv.reader** function aren't useable yet. You have to loop through the data stored in **contents_of_f**, line by line, adding each line to a list.

Here's the code:

```
1 with open("competitions.csv") as f:
2    reader_of_f = csv.reader(f)
3    potter_competitions = []
4    for each_line in contents_of_f:
5      potter_competitions += each_line
```

First, you define **potter_competitions** as an empty list:

```
1 with open("competitions.csv") as f:
2    contents_of_f = csv.reader(f)
3    potter_competitions = []
4    for each_line in contents_of_f:
5      potter_competitions += each_line
```

Then comes the loop:

```
1 with open("competitions.csv") as f:
2    contents_of_f = csv.reader(f)
3    potter_competitions = []
4    for each_line in contents_of_f:
5      potter_competitions += each_line
```

The loop appends each line of the CSV file to the

potter_competitions list. When the loop ends, the list is complete:

```
1 with open("competitions.csv") as f:
2    contents_of_f = csv.reader(f)
3    potter_competitions = []
4    for each_line in contents_of_f:
5        potter_competitions += each_line
```

If you write…

```
print(potter_competitions)
```

…Python displays the list…

['Year', 'Event', 'Winner', '1995', 'Best-Kept Lawn', 'None', '1999', 'Gobstones', 'Welch National', '2006', 'World Cup', 'Burkina Faso']

Find the interactive coding exercises for this chapter at: http://www.ASmarterWayToLearn.com/python/68.html

69

CSV files: Picking information out of them

We exported an Excel spreadsheet…

	A	B	C
1	**Year**	**Event**	**Winner**
2	1995	Best-Kept Lawn	None
3	1999	Gobstones	Welch National
4	2006	World Cup	Burkina Faso

…into a CSV file named *competitions.csv*…

```
Year,Event,Winner
1995,Best-Kept Lawn,None
1999,Gobstones,Welch Nationional
2006,World Cup,Burkina Faso
```

Using a function of the Python **cvs** module called **reader**, we read the contents of the file. Looping through it line-by-line, we translated the contents into a Python list named **potter_competitions**:

['Year', 'Event', 'Winner', '1995', 'Best-Kept Lawn', 'None', '1999', 'Gobstones', 'Welch National', '2006', 'World Cup', 'Burkina Faso']

Suppose a user wants to enter the name of a competition to find out the winner. We can use the list to do that.

We'll need a Python method that's new to you.

You've learned how to find an element in a list by specifying its index number. For example, in the list named **potter_competitions**, if you write…

```
print(potter_competitions[4])
```

…Python displays…

Best-Kept Lawn

There's also a method for *finding* the index number of an element. If you write…

```
index_number_of_target = potter_competitions.index("Best-Kept Lawn")
```

…Python looks through the list and finds that the index number of "Best-Kept Lawn" is 4.

> Year,Event,Winner
> 1995,**Best-Kept Lawn**,None
> 1999,Gobstones,Welch Nationional
> 2006,World Cup,Burkina Faso

The number is stored in the variable named `index_number_of_target`.

Let's say the user wants to know the winner of the Best-Kept Lawn competition.

We begin by finding the index number of "Best-Kept Lawn" in the list—4.

> Year,Event,Winner
> 1995,**Best-Kept Lawn**,None
> 1999,Gobstones,Welch Nationional
> 2006,World Cup,Burkina Faso

Then, knowing the winner of that competition is the next element in the list, we can look it up by specifying an index number that's one more than the index number of the competition—5.

> Year,Event,Winner
> 1995,Best-Kept Lawn,**None**
> 1999,Gobstones,Welch Nationional
> 2006,World Cup,Burkina Faso

The element with an index number of 5 is **None**.

Line 1 gets the user's input and stores it in the variable named `target`:

```
1 target = input("Enter the name of a competition: ")
2 index_number_of_target =
potter_competitions.index(target)
3 index_number_of_winner = index_number_of_target + 1
4 the_winner = potter_competitions[index_number_of_winner]
5 print("The winner was " + the_winner)
```

Line 2 looks up the index number of the string stored in **target** and stores that index number in the variable named **index_number_of_target**:

```
1 target = input("Enter the name of a competition: ")
2 index_number_of_target =
potter_competitions.index(target)
3 index_number_of_winner = index_number_of_target + 1
4 the_winner = potter_competitions[index_number_of_winner]
5 print("The winner was " + the_winner)
```

Line 3 adds 1 to the index number of the competition. This is the index number of the winner. It is stored in the variable named **index_number_of_winner**:

```
1 target = input("Enter the name of a competition: ")
2 index_number_of_target =
potter_competitions.index(target)
3 index_number_of_winner = index_number_of_target + 1
4 the_winner = potter_competitions[index_number_of_winner]
5 print("The winner was " + the_winner)
```

Line 4 looks up the name of the winner and stores it in the variable named **the_winner**:

```
1 target = input("Enter the name of a competition: ")
2 index_number_of_target =
potter_competitions.index(target)
3 index_number_of_winner = index_number_of_target + 1
4 the_winner = potter_competitions[index_number_of_winner]
5 print("The winner was " + the_winner)
```

Line 5 displays the name of the winner:

```
1 target = input("Enter the name of a competition: ")
2 index_number_of_target =
potter_competitions.index(target)
3 index_number_of_winner = index_number_of_target + 1
4 the_winner = potter_competitions[index_number_of_winner]
5 print("The winner was " + the_winner)
```

If the user has entered "Best-Kept Lawn," the code finds that its index number is 4, looks up the element whose index number is 5, and displays…

The winner was None

Find the interactive coding exercises for this chapter at: http://www.ASmarterWayToLearn.com/python/69.html

70
CSV files: Loading information into them.
Part 1

The *csv* module contains a function that reads a CSV file. It also contains a function that allows you to write to a CSV file.

You start by importing the module:

```
1 import csv
```

If you've already imported the *csv* module for some other operation, you don't have to do it again.

Then you open (or create) the file:

```
1 import csv
2 with open("whatever.csv", "w", newline="") as f:
```

This statement opens a file so you can write to it. The statement is similar to the code you learned to open a text file for writing. It begins **with open**...

```
2 with open("whatever.csv", "w", newline="") as f:
```

...then the name of the file...

```
2 with open("whatever.csv", "w", newline="") as f:
```

...then "w" in quotation marks...

```
2 with open("whatever.csv", "w", newline="") as f:
```

And you specify a file handle at the end. Again, I've chosen to call it **f**...

```
2 with open("whatever.csv", "w", newline="") as f:
```

Here's something new: **newline=""**.

```
2 with open("whatever.csv", "w", newline="") as f:
```

newline="" is a technical requirement. At this point, there's no need to understand it. Just remember to include it.

Also important to remember:
If there's no such file as the file you specify…

```
2 with open("whatever.csv", "w", newline="") as f:
```

…Python will create the file.

If the file already exists, any information already in it will be overwritten by the new information that you're loading into it. Later I'll show you how to append information to an existing file, preserving any information that's already in it.

Find the interactive coding exercises for this chapter at:
http://www.ASmarterWayToLearn.com/python/70.html

71
CSV files: Loading information into them.
Part 2

At some point in your code you've imported the *csv* module. And you've opened a CVS file (or created it if it doesn't already exist):

```
with open("whatever.csv", "w", newline="") as f:
```

Now you call the **writer** function in the *csv* module:

```
1 with open("whatever.csv", "w", newline="") as f:
2   data_handler = csv.writer(…
```

For technical reasons, you can't write data directly to the CSV file. You have to create a special object that handles the data. You begin line 2 by creating this object. Use any legal variable name:

```
1 with open("whatever.csv", "w", newline="") as f:
2   data_handler = csv.writer(…
```

Next, an equal sign…

```
1 with open("whatever.csv", "w", newline="") as f:
2   data_handler = csv.writer(…
```

Then the file handle from line 1…

```
1 with open("whatever.csv", "w", newline="") as f:
2   data_handler = csv.writer(f…
```

Finally, you tell Python what you're using as a delimiter:

```
1 with open("whatever.csv", "w", newline="") as f:
2   data_handler = csv.writer(f, delimiter=",")
```

The reason you have to specify a delimiter is that, although CSV files are named for *comma*-separated values, the separators, or delimiters, can be tabs, semicolons, pipes (|), or carets (^). So you need to tell Python which one to use.

Find the interactive coding exercises for this chapter at:
http://www.ASmarterWayToLearn.com/python/71.html

72
CSV files: Loading information into them.
Part 3

We've opened the file *competitions.csv* (or created it if it doesn't already exist). We've told Python we're opening the file to write to it. And we've called the function:

```
1 with open("whatever.csv", "w", newline="") as f:
2   data_handler = csv.writer(f, delimiter=",")
```

Now we write some rows of data to the file, one row at a time:

```
1 with open("whatever.csv", "w", newline="") as f:
2   data_handler = csv.writer(f, delimiter=",")
3   data_handler.writerow(["Year", "Event", "Winner"])
4   data_handler.writerow(["1995", "Best-Kept Lawn",
"None"])
5   data_handler.writerow(["1999", "Gobstones", "Welch
National"])
```

If we open *whatever.csv* in Excel or another spreadsheet app, it looks like this:

	A	B	C
1	Year	Event	Winner
2	1995	Best-Kept Lawn	None
3	1999	Gobstones	Welch National

Things to remember:

It's the variable **data_handler** connected by a dot to the keyword **writerow**...

```
3    data_handler.writerow(["Year", "Event", "Winner"])
4    data_handler.writerow(["1995", "Best-Kept Lawn",
"None"])
5    data_handler.writerow(["1999", "Gobstones", "Welch
National"])
```

Each row is loaded into the handler as a list:

```
3    data_handler.writerow(["Year", "Event", "Winner"])
4    data_handler.writerow(["1995", "Best-Kept Lawn",
"None"])
5    data_handler.writerow(["1999", "Gobstones", "Welch
National"])
```

Find the interactive coding exercises for this chapter at:
http://www.ASmarterWayToLearn.com/python/72.html

73
CSV files: Appending rows to them.

In previous chapters you learned that the **cvs.writer** function wipes out any existing data in a CSV file and replaces it with the rows that you write to it. But this happens only if you specify **"w"** in the line that opens the file…

```
1 with open("whatever.csv", "w", newline="") as f:
```

If you specify **"a"** instead…

```
1 with open("whatever.csv", "a", newline="") as f:
```

…you can append new data, preserving the data that's already in the file…

```
1 with open("whatever.csv", "a", newline="") as f:
2   data_handler = csv.writer(f, delimiter=",")
3   data_handler.writerow(["2006", "World Cup", "Burkina
Faso"])
4   data_handler.writerow(["2011", "Butter Cup", "France"])
5   data_handler.writerow(["2012", "Coffee Cup", "Brazil"])
```

Now the CSV file, which originally had three rows, looks like this when you open it in Excel:

	A	B	C
1	Year	Event	Winner
2	1995	Best-Kept Lawn	None
3	1999	Gobstones	Welch National
4	2006	World Cup	Burkina Faso
5	2011	Butter Cup	France
6	2012	Coffee Cup	Brazil

Find the interactive coding exercises for this chapter at:

http://www.ASmarterWayToLearn.com/python/73.html

74
How to save a Python list or dictionary in a file: JSON

In an earlier chapter you learned how to save text in a file...

```
1 with open("greet.txt", "w") as f:
2   f.write("Hello, world!")
```

...and how to retrieve the text from the file...

```
1 with open("greet.txt", "r") as f:
2   text_of_file = f.read()
```

Then if you write...

```
print(text_of_file)
```

...Python displays...

Hello, World!

Now suppose you want to save something besides a text string. Let's say you want to save a Python list.

```
1 alphabet_letters = ["a", "b", "c"]
2 with open("alphabet_list.txt", "w") as f:
3   f.write(alphabet_letters)
```

The code above produces an error message:

TypeError: write() argument must be str, not list

You can't save a Python list in a text file. You can only save a text string.

You *can* save a list in a CSV file, but a more straightforward approach is to use JSON. The four characters stand for **JavaScript Object Notation**. As the name suggests, it was created for JavaScript developers. But Python coders can use it, too.

It's pronounced JAY-sun.

The *json* module is included in the Python 3 package that you've installed on your computer. You begin by importing it:

```
import json
```

You've defined a list:

```
1 alphabet_letters = ["a", "b", "c"]
```

To save the list, you open a file as usual (creating it if it doesn't exist):

```
1 alphabet_letters = ["a", "b", "c"]
2 with open("alphabet_list.json", "w") as f:
```

The next line writes the list to the file:

```
1 alphabet_letters = ["a", "b", "c"]
2 with open("alphabet_list.json", "w") as f:
3     json.dump(alphabet_letters, f)
```

The line begins with the name of the module...

```
1 alphabet_letters = ["a", "b", "c"]
2 with open("alphabet_list.json", "w") as f:
3     json.dump(alphabet_letters, f)
```

Then comes a dot followed by the name of the function we're calling, **dump**...

```
1 alphabet_letters = ["a", "b", "c"]
2 with open("alphabet_list.json", "w") as f:
3     json.dump(alphabet_letters, f)
```

The function call takes two arguments, the variable name of the list we're storing ...

```
1 alphabet_letters = ["a", "b", "c"]
2 with open("alphabet_list.json", "w") as f:
3     json.dump(alphabet_letters, f)
```

...and the file handle we've assigned for the file where we're storing the list...

```
1 alphabet_letters = ["a", "b", "c"]
2 with open("alphabet_list.json", "w") as f:
3   json.dump(alphabet_letters, f)
```

If you've defined a dictionary...

```
1 customer_29876 = {
2   "first name": "David",
3   "last name": "Elliott",
4   "address": "4803 Wellesley St.",
5 }
```

...you save it the same way:

```
1 with open("customer_29876.json", "w") as f:
2   json.dump(customer_29876, f)
```

Find the interactive coding exercises for this chapter at:
http://www.ASmarterWayToLearn.com/python/74.html

75

How to retrieve a Python list or dictionary from a JSON file

In the last chapter, you learned how to save a Python list or dictionary in a file using the *json* module.

This is the dictionary:

```
1 customer_29876 = {
2   "first name": "David",
3   "last name": "Elliott",
4   "address": "4803 Wellesley St.",
5 }
```

You saved the dictionary in a file called **customer_29876.json**. Now you want to retrieve it.

I'm assuming you've already imported the *json* module. If you haven't, you'd do that.

You begin by opening the file for reading, as usual:

```
1 with open("customer_29876.json") as f:
2   customer_29876 = json.load(f)
```

Then you call the **load** function of the **json** module, specifying the file handle I've assigned to **customer_29876.json**, **f**. The dictionary is retrieved and stored in the variable I've named **customer_29876**.

```
1 with open("customer_29876.json") as f:
2   customer_29876 = json.load(f)
```

If you write…

```
print(customer_29876)
```

…Python displays the dictionary that you saved in the file and have now retrieved…

{'first name': 'David', 'last name': 'Elliott', 'address': '4803 Wellesley St.'}

If you write…

```
print(customer_29876["last name"])
```

…Python displays…

Elliott

In this chapter, we've retrieved a Python dictionary saved in a JSON file. You'd use the same syntax to retrieve a Python list saved in a JSON file.

Find the interactive coding exercises for this chapter at:
http://www.ASmarterWayToLearn.com/python/75.html

76
Planning for things to go wrong

Bad things can happen to good programs. For example, your program invites the user to enter the name of a file so she can access some information...

```
1 filename = input("What text file to open? ")
2 with open(filename) as f:
3   print(f.read())
```

Line 1 of the code above asks the user for the name of a text file and assigns her answer to the variable **filename**. Line 2 opens the file. Line 3 reads the file and displays the contents.

What do you suppose happens if the user enters the name of a file that doesn't exist? Python stops cold, displaying this user-unfriendly message:

FileNotFoundError: [Errno 2] No such file or directory: 'abc.txt'

Reading this message, the user *may* be able to figure out what the problem is. But it doesn't matter, because the program is no longer working.

When things go wrong, it doesn't have to be fatal, if you code an *exception*. This gives the user a clearer error message and also keeps the program from shutting down.

Here's how to adapt the code above:

```
1 try:
2   filename = input("What text file to open? ")
3   with open(filename) as f:
4     print(f.read())
5 except FileNotFoundError:
6   print("Sorry, " + filename + " not found.")
```

Lines 1 through 4 say, "Try getting a filename from the user, opening it, and displaying its contents." Lines 5 and 6 say, "If there's no such file, display a message, then carry on."

Note the syntax.

The code under **try:** is indented…

```
1 try:
2   filename = input("What text file to open? ")
3   with open(filename) as f:
4     print(f.read())
5 except FileNotFoundError:
6   print("Sorry, " + filename + " not found.")
```

Line 5 begins with the keyword **except**, followed by the keyword **FileNotFoundError** and a colon…

```
1 try:
2   filename = input("What text file to open? ")
3   with open(filename) as f:
4     print(f.read())
5 except FileNotFoundError:
6   print("Sorry, " + filename + " not found.")
```

The line under the **except** statement is indented…

```
1 try:
2   filename = input("What text file to open? ")
3   with open(filename) as f:
4     print(f.read())
5 except FileNotFoundError:
6   print("Sorry, " + filename + " not found.")
```

FileNotFoundError is just one of dozens of errors you can handle gracefully using **try** and **except**. Find a complete list of errors at https://docs.python.org/3/library/exceptions.html.

Find the interactive coding exercises for this chapter at: http://www.ASmarterWayToLearn.com/python/76.html

77
A more practical example of exception handling

In the last chapter, we used **try** and **except** to handle a
FileNotFoundError if the user entered the name of a nonexistent
file. The code displayed a meaningful error message and kept the
program from dying. But normally, we would want to give the user
another try after he inputs a filename for a file that can't be found. For
this, we need a **while** loop:

```
1 while True:
2    try:
3      filename = input("What text file to open? ")
4      with open(filename) as f:
5        print(f.read())
6        break
7    except FileNotFoundError:
8      print("Sorry, " + filename + " not found.")
```

The code above says, "If the **FileNotFoundError** occurs (line 7),
display the error message (line 8) and try again (line 2). If the file opens
(line 4), display its contents (line 5), and break out of the **while** loop
(line 6).

A reminder: For practical purposes, **while True** means, "Keep
repeating the following statements until there's a **break** statement." As
long as the user's input causes an error, there's no **break** statement,
and the code keeps going back to line 3. When the user's input results in
Python successfully opening a file, the **print** statement executes and
the **break** statement ends the loop.

Note the indents. As usual, every block of code that takes its orders
from a line above is indented one level beyond the line above.

Find the interactive coding exercises for this chapter at:
http://www.ASmarterWayToLearn.com/python/77.html

Guide to the appendices

Appendix A - An easy way to run Python

Appendix B - How to install Python on your computer

Appendix C - How to run Python in the terminal

Appendix D - How to create a Python program
that you can save

Appendix E - How to run a saved Python program in the terminal

Appendix A
An easy way to run Python

There are many ways to run your Python code. For starters, you can run your code in an online simulator.

The simulator I like is Trinket.

In the final exercises for each chapter, you've been running your code in Trinket:

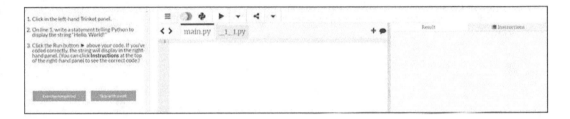

You can use Trinket yourself to run any Python code you like. Just sign up for a Trinket account at https://trinket.io

The account is free if you are okay with using Python 2. This book teaches the more recent version, Python 3, but the two versions are similar. My recommendation is to sign up for a free account and take Trinket for a road test. If you get serious about Python, you might want to upgrade to a paid Trinket Connect account. It enables Python 3 and costs $9 per month or $72 per year.

Appendix B
How to install Python on your computer

When the Python interpreter sees **`print("Hello, world!")`**, it translates the text into a computer instruction and commands the computer to execute it. The computer displays **Hello, World!** on the screen.

But it won't happen without the Python interpreter.

An easy way to run Python is to use an online simulator that incorporates a Python interpreter, like Trinket, at at https://trinket.io. (See Appendix A.)

However, if you want to run Python on your computer, you need to have the Python interpreter installed on your computer.

Windows doesn't come with Python preinstalled. You need to download it and install it on your computer. It's free.

Macs do come with Python preinstalled, but at this writing, the preinstalled version is Python 2.7, not the Python 3 that I'm teaching. Most of the Python syntax you're learning here works with Python 2.7, but not all of it. You can upgrade to Python 3, free.

Linux comes with Python installed. Recent Linux releases include Python 3, but not necessarily the latest version. An earlier version of Python 3 is fine for our purposes.

Python 3 is best for learning and for building new applications, but you may need Python 2 if you're going to be working on existing programs that someone else has created. You can install both versions on your computer and switch between them. But here I'm focusing on Python 3.

I've posted online instructions for downloading and installing Python 3 on your Windows, Mac, or Linux computer.

Install Python 3 for Windows

Go to http://www.ASmarterWayToLearn.com/python/python-for-windows.html

Install Python 3 for a Mac

Go to http://www.ASmarterWayToLearn.com/python/python-for-mac.html

Install Python 3 for Linux

Go to http://www.ASmarterWayToLearn.com/python/python-for-linux.html

Appendix C
How to run Python in the terminal

Your operating system comes with a terminal application. Among other things, the terminal lets you enter Python code and run the code. (This is true only if you have Python installed on your computer. If you don't have it installed, see Appendix B.)

Note: In Windows, the terminal is called PowerShell.

The terminal is good for writing and running small Python snippets. Since there's no straightforward way tot save the code that you write in the terminal, you wouldn't use it to write a full Python program.

Open the Windows terminal (PowerShell)
Go to http://www.ASmarterWayToLearn.com/python/open-terminal-windows.html

Open the terminal on a Mac
Go to http://www.ASmarterWayToLearn.com/python/open-terminal-mac.html

Open the Linux terminal
Go to http://www.ASmarterWayToLearn.com/python/open-terminal-linux.html

Let's write and run some Python. I'll demonstrate using Windows PowerShell.

1 In Windows, enter **python**. On a Mac, enter **python3**. In Linux, enter **python3.6** (or whatever the latest version that you've installed is).

2 Try it. Enter **print("hi")**

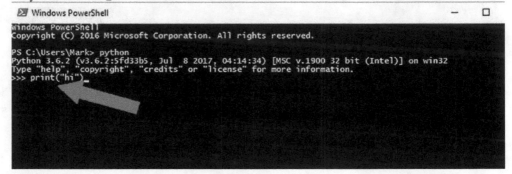

When you press **Enter**, your Python code executes. **Hi** displays. And you get a new prompt so you can enter another Python command if you like.

3 You can write multi-line code in the terminal. Try it. Start by writing **greet = "hi"** and press **Enter**.

```
Windows PowerShell                                          —    □
Windows PowerShell
Copyright (C) 2016 Microsoft Corporation. All rights reserved.

PS C:\Users\Mark> python
Python 3.6.2 (v3.6.2:5fd33b5, Jul  8 2017, 04:14:34) [MSC v.1900 32 bit (Intel)] on win32
Type "help", "copyright", "credits" or "license" for more information.
>>> print("hi")
hi
>>> greet = "hi"
>>> _
```

4 Now write **if greet == "hi":** and press **Enter**. Notice that you get a new type of prompt—three dots. This tells you to indent the next line.

```
Windows PowerShell                                          —    □
Windows PowerShell
Copyright (C) 2016 Microsoft Corporation. All rights reserved.

PS C:\Users\Mark> python
Python 3.6.2 (v3.6.2:5fd33b5, Jul  8 2017, 04:14:34) [MSC v.1900 32 bit (Intel)] on win32
Type "help", "copyright", "credits" or "license" for more information.
>>> print("hi")
hi
>>> greet = "hi"
>>> if greet == "hi":
...
```

5 At the three-dot prompt, press **Tab** to indent. Then write **print(greet)**. Press **Enter**. Notice that you get another three-dot prompt. This is in case you want to add another instruction based on the **if** condition being met. You don't. So press **Enter** once more.

```
Windows PowerShell                                          —    □
Windows PowerShell
Copyright (C) 2016 Microsoft Corporation. All rights reserved.

PS C:\Users\Mark> python
Python 3.6.2 (v3.6.2:5fd33b5, Jul  8 2017, 04:14:34) [MSC v.1900 32 bit (Intel)] on win32
Type "help", "copyright", "credits" or "license" for more information.
>>> print("hi")
hi
>>> greet = "hi"
>>> if greet == "hi":
...     print(greet)
...
```

6 **Hi** displays. And you get a new **>>>** prompt.

```
Windows PowerShell                                                    —    □

Windows PowerShell
Copyright (C) 2016 Microsoft Corporation. All rights reserved.

PS C:\Users\Mark> python
Python 3.6.2 (v3.6.2:5fd33b5, Jul  8 2017, 04:14:34) [MSC v.1900 32 bit (Intel)] on win32
Type "help", "copyright", "credits" or "license" for more information.
>>> print("hi")
hi
>>> greet = "hi"
>>> if greet == "hi":
...     print(greet)
...
hi
>>>
```

7 To close Python, enter **exit()**. Python closes, and you're
returned to the original terminal prompt.

```
Windows PowerShell                                                    —    □

Windows PowerShell
Copyright (C) 2016 Microsoft Corporation. All rights reserved.

PS C:\Users\Mark> python
Python 3.6.2 (v3.6.2:5fd33b5, Jul  8 2017, 04:14:34) [MSC v.1900 32 bit (Intel)] on win32
Type "help", "copyright", "credits" or "license" for more information.
>>> print("hi")
hi
>>> greet = "hi"
>>> if greet == "hi":
...     print(greet)
...
hi
>>> exit()
PS C:\Users\Mark> _
```

Appendix D
How to create a Python program
that you can save

A Python program is just a text file with a file name ending in the file extension **.py** (for Python). If you open a text editor and write...

```
print("Hello world")
```

...and you save that as, say, **greeting.py**, that's a Python program.

If you open a text editor and write ten thousand lines of Python and you save it as, say **save_the_world.py**, that's a Python program.

When I say text editor, I mean a writing application that's not a word processing program like Microsoft Word. Word processing programs format text. Text editors don't format. Text editors produce pure, unformatted text. A Python program must be pure text without formatting.

In Windows, you can create Python programs using the Notepad text editor that comes preinstalled with Windows. On a Mac, you can write Python programs using TextEdit (in plain text mode) that comes with a Mac.

Most serious coders use specialized text editors that include convenience features for programming. According to a Sitepoint survey, the four most popular editors for Python programming are:

1. **Sublime Text.** Works with Windows, Mac, and Ubuntu (Linux). Free to try for an indefinite period (with reminders to buy), $70 for a single user.

2. **Vim.** Included free with Mac and most Linux systems. A version for Windows is free.

3. **Emacs.** Included free with most Linux systems. Windows and Mac versions are free. Installation for these operating systems is complicated.

4. **Notepad++.** Works only with Windows. Free.

These specialized editors, and many others, can be downloaded from their respective websites.

Another option is IDLE (**I**ntegrated **D**evelopment and **L**earning **E**nvironment). IDLE is more than a text editor, but includes a text editor. As *Learning* in the name suggests, IDLE is a good tool for learning Python. I'm going to show you how to use it.

IDLE is bundled with Python 3. If you've installed Python 3 on your computer, you've also got IDLE on your computer.

Let's check to be sure that you *do* have Python 3 on your computer, and that it will load without a lot of fuss.

Check for Python 3 on Windows
Follow the instructions at
http://www.ASmarterWayToLearn.com/python/check-install-python-for-windows.html

Check for Python 3 on a Mac
Follow the instructions at
http://www.ASmarterWayToLearn.com/python/check-install-python-for-mac.html

Check for Python 3 on Linux
Follow the instructions at
http://www.ASmarterWayToLearn.com/python/check-install-python-for-linux.html

If the test doesn't succeed, Python 3 may or may not be on your computer somewhere. You could spend some time looking for it, but it may be simpler to just install it fresh.

Install Python 3 on Windows

Go to http://www.ASmarterWayToLearn.com/python/python-for-windows.html

Install Python 3 on a Mac

Go to http://www.ASmarterWayToLearn.com/python/python-for-mac.html

Install Python 3 for Linux

Go to http://www.ASmarterWayToLearn.com/python/python-for-linux.html

With Python 3 installed on your computer, you're ready to fire up IDLE.

Run IDLE on Windows

Go to http://www.ASmarterWayToLearn.com/python/IDLE-for-windows.html

Run IDLE on a Mac

Go to http://www.ASmarterWayToLearn.com/python/IDLE-for-mac.html

Run IDLE on Linux

Go to http://www.ASmarterWayToLearn.com/python/IDLE-for-linux.html

Appendix E
How to run a saved Python program in the terminal

Let's say you've saved your program **greet.py**. Now you want to run it. If you're using IDLE, you could run it in IDLE. But maybe you're using a text editor that, unlike IDLE, doesn't include a shell that runs Python programs.

So you'll run the program in the terminal.

Open the Windows terminal (PowerShell)
Go to http://www.ASmarterWayToLearn.com/python/open-terminal-windows.html

Open the terminal on a Mac
Go to http://www.ASmarterWayToLearn.com/python/open-terminal-mac.html

Open the Linux terminal
Go to http://www.ASmarterWayToLearn.com/python/open-terminal-linux.html

I'll demonstrate using Windows PowerShell.

1 Begin by changing the active directory to the directory in which you saved your Python file. The instructions in Appendix D asked you to save your Python file in the **Desktop** folder. If you followed those directions, enter **cd Desktop**. If your Python file is in another directory and you're not sure how to get to it in the terminal, go to http://www.digitalcitizen.life/command-prompt-how-use-basic-commands

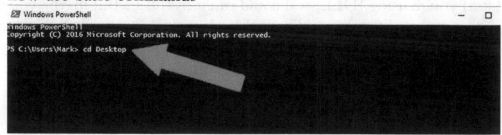

The active Directory is now **Desktop**.

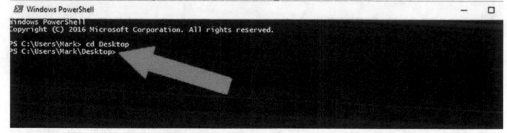

2 In Windows, enter **python greet.py**. On a Mac and in Linux, enter **python3 greet.py**.

Python displays the string **Hi**.

```
Windows PowerShell                                                    —    □
Windows PowerShell
Copyright (C) 2016 Microsoft Corporation. All rights reserved.

PS C:\Users\Mark> python
Python 3.6.2 (v3.6.2:5fd33b5, Jul  8 2017, 04:14:34) [MSC v.1900 32 bit (Intel)] on win32
Type "help", "copyright", "credits" or "license" for more information.
>>> print("hi")
hi
>>>
```

Printed in the USA
CPSIA information can be obtained
at www.ICGtesting.com
LVHW080257251023
762013LV00006B/798